white screens
black images

white screens
black images

Hollywood
from the
Dark Side

James Snead edited by Colin MacCabe & Cornel West

Routledge · New York & London

Published in 1994 by

Routledge
29 West 35 Street
New York, NY 10001

Published in Great Britain by
Routledge
11 New Fetter Lane
London EC4P 4EE

Printed in the United States of America on acid free paper.

The Publishers gratefully acknowledge the assistance of Terry Geesken
and the Film Stills Archive of the Museum of Modern Art in providing the
illustrations for this volume.

Library of Congress and British Library Cataloguing in Publication data is
available.

ISBN 0-415-90573-7 (HB)
ISBN 0-415-90574-5 (PB)

Contents

Foreword

Colin MacCabe

James Snead died on March 26, 1989 in Pittsburgh. In my last conversation with him, and when I was completely unaware of the terminal nature of his illness, he said, a propos of the fact that he had had to abandon the teaching for the term, "One good thing about this illness is that I am going to get both books finished". The books he was referring to were the history of black representation in American cinema on which he had been working for the previous three years and a book on African-American culture which he was writing with Cornel West and which the three of us had discussed in a memorable all night session the previous year in Philadelphia. When James died both I and his brother George, to whom he had spoken at much greater length and who he had charged with the responsibility to ensure the posthumous publication, were overwhelmed by the state of Jamie's papers and computer files.

The volume of work accomplished by someone who was only thirty five at his death and who had spent (unusually for an academic) a couple of years working as a banker for Chase Manhattan was simply staggering. Four novels, numerous short stories, papers and lectures without end—and all this in addition to the published work on Faulkner. However, there was not, as we had both been expecting, two books almost ready for the printers. Of the planned collaboration with Cornel West there were only the merest traces. Of the book on American black cinema, there was too much and too little. Too much in the sense that there were three or four versions of each chapter. Too little in the sense that there was no definite outline of the book and no clear sense of James's own priorities in the versions of the chapters he had left. Indeed the best indication of the book James had planned was a version that he had given me a year earlier. What then began was a long editorial process which, in different geographical circumstances, would have been much shorter. George Snead and the physical material were in Los Angeles, Cornel West on the East Coast and I was split between Pittsburgh and Europe. A first collation, with the three of us, was attempted in February 1990 in Los Angeles. More work was carried out by Cornel West and George Snead that autumn and a final version and a division of responsibility for the introduction arrived at by Cornel West and myself in the extraordinarily unlikely setting of Reno, Nevada in September 1991. The editorial process was completed by a diligent and talented copy editor at Routledge.

The text of the book that one can now read is not the text that James would have himself approved. The arguments of the second half of the book would have been worked into a continuous text and there would have been a very full illustration of all the arguments through impeccably researched stills. Nonetheless I feel confident that in this book one can read Jamie's major arguments: the centrality of black representation to a history of Hollywood, a refusal to read that representation as merely positive or negative and a linked determination to read it in relation to the deepest of political and sexual fantasies. There are, however, two omissions which must be noted. The first is, apart from one or two sentences, a lack of any material on the blaxploitation genre (*Shaft*, *Superfly*) of the early seventies. Any attempt to give a general history of black representation in America would have to deal with this first Hollywood reaction to black power, which appeared to code certain blacks positively while establishing that definition within a cripplingly limited and stereotypical view of the ghetto. This absence is not of crucial importance—it is clear how to develop Snead's analysis to deal with what was never more than a relatively minor genre. The second absence is both more important and absolutely inevitable. Spike Lee's *Do The Right Thing* premiered at Cannes a mere two months after James's death and the last three years have seen an explosion of films by black directors, financed by the mainstream. James's death robbed these films of the one intellectual who was really prepared for their arrival and it seems to me that it is impossible to read his reaction to them from the terms that he develops in this book. Indeed this book should have been part of the cultural context into which these films first appeared. Instead it will appear in the aftermath of that first wave which culminated in John Singleton's *BoyzN The Hood*. One can only hope that it will contribute to the debate about them; the debate that Snead foresaw when he wrote:

> "It will be interesting to see in the coming years whether the oppositional aesthetics and thematics of their earlier 'independent' films can be adapted for mass-market consumption. Some would doubt whether white Americans can ever learn to see blacks and themselves from a black, and not a white, vantage point. . . . Perhaps the greatest challenge for future black filmmakers, independent or not, is to find a way to prevent an imagistic co-optation in which an insincere, ritualized tolerance of recoded images may itself become just another way of keeping blacks out of the picture." (p. 119)

It is certain that the debate will go on without James Snead but it is also certain, and this gives a real idea of Jamie's stature, that the debate will be missing a crucial voice. In this age of ever increasing specialization it is important to recognize that Snead was not a specialist in film studies. His scholarly interest in film came about because in 1985 Cornel West was invited to give a lecture about black film which he felt unable to attend. As Cornel himself said in his memorial lecture delivered at Pittsburgh in April 1989, the invitation was itself a sign of the critical scarcity of black intellectuals—so that those that do exist are constantly being asked to comment on areas outside their specialization. Cornel, however, suggested that Jamie take up the invitation and it took very little time for him to see the scholarly and intellectual challenge offered by the whole question of blacks and cinema. While important empirical pioneers had opened up the field in the seventies, they had opened it up using very simplistic forms of analysis in terms of positive and negative images. They had not used the crucial terms of cultural analysis developed from the insights of French thinkers like Roland Barthes and Jacques Derrida. For Snead the first crucial step was to recognize the structuralist insight that all signs can only be defined diacritically—and thus that any analysis of race must recognize that any definition of black always involves definitions of white. The second and complementary step was to adopt the post-structuralist perspective that diacritical definitions were always in process—articulated in a perpetual process of signification where it was impossible to isolate the couplet black/white without further examining its ramifications in relation to other fundamental distinctions, particularly sexual ones.

What Snead saw quickly was that the cinema, the major cultural form of the twentieth century, bore eloquent witness to W. E. B. DuBois's claim that the 'Negro' is the central metaphor of the 20th century and this book is nothing more nor less than the investigation of how that metaphor was deployed in the cinema to articulate the unconscious bases of the power relationships embodied in master/slave, civilized/primitive, good/evil. In these days of easy academic superlatives, in which every assistant professor is an outstanding scholar making a groundbreaking contribution to our knowledge, it is difficult to find the terms which convey the power of Jamie's intellect, the ferocity of his industry, his absolute commitment to the life of the mind. To many it will be surprising, indeed difficult to believe, that someone could master both the theoretical terms of film theory and the history of Hollywood so quickly but one should not underestimate the speed at which Jamie could work nor the genuine mastery that he could achieve.

As his Ph.D. supervisor at Cambridge I was the last person to so underestimate him. He first burst into my life at Cambridge in an absolute rage. He had arrived in Cambridge, as many American students before him, to discover that he was expected to spend his two years there completing another undergraduate degree (the Part 2 of the English Tripos). To someone as ambitious, in every sense of the term, as Jamie, such marking time was almost criminal. He therefore besieged the administrative instances of the English faculty and they, surprisingly, (but Jamie was very black, very big, and very mad at the thought of wasting two years) said that he could indeed register as a Ph.D. student if he could find a member of the faculty willing to supervise him. He arrived in my office having already being turned down by a number of my more cautious colleagues. I immediately asked him if I could look at some of his work and he gave me his Scholar of the House dissertation from Yale on Mann and Joyce. When I read it I was astonished both by his grasp of literary modernism but also by his profound philosophical culture, by his intimate understanding of Hegel and Nietzsche. I had no hesitation in accepting him as a pupil because, by my own reckoning, his undergraduate work was, staggeringly, already of doctoral standard. However, I was more concerned about the topic. He himself wanted to continue his work on Joyce and Mann but I was against that for a number of reasons. I felt that he had to a large extent already mastered European modernism and that his doctorate would thus just repeat reading he had already accomplished but also that a great deal of work was currently being published on these topics (including my own book on Joyce). More importantly I felt very strongly that if the power of poststructuralist reading was to indicate more than its own virtuosity, it was important to anchor those readings in real historical contradiction and I therefore suggested to him that he consider Faulkner. Not only was *Absalom! Absalom!* the great modernist text which had received relatively little critical attention but in Faulkner the paradoxes of modernist writing were integrally linked to questions of race. It was at this point that I was made aware of the truly phenomenal nature of Jamie's appetite for work. Within a few months he had not only read through the entire Faulkner corpus with an intensity of attention which made every line yield up its formal strategies as well as its content but he had also worked his way through the secondary Faulkner literature and made a very good start on the contextual history and sociology. In the thesis, in which Faulkner was linked to Joyce, and in the subsequent book which concentrated purely on Faulkner, Jamie read the modernist disruption of representation around the impossibility of and necessity to establish difference in the world. His work showed clearly how Faulkner is intent in engaging his readers in the problem of representation, the very process of differentiation through which we divide the world into identities. The racial segregation of the South is overlaid on sexual difference to provide both style and theme of the books—with an incestuous miscegenation constantly threatening to ruin all identities both linguistic and social. One of the troubling emphases of this work is to suggest that racial oppression is simply the most appalling and evident example of a process endemic to any form of representation which must always divide in order to identify.

This fundamental philosophical theme is one that runs through the work on Faulkner, pitting Plato against the pre-Socratics and Nietzsche, showing how the Platonic emphasis on identity is unable to solve the paradoxes of representation. It is these paradoxes which Faulkner dramatizes again and again—identity is only ever the product of a difference which renders identity constitutionally unstable. Race then becomes both form and content for Faulkner, the necessity to separate black and white becoming sexually, socially and linguistically the neuralgic and impossible centres of his work.

The authority with which Snead deploys his grasp of both the Western philosophical tradition and the historical reality of modernism is astonishing but the political force of the book is often pessimistic. Snead is absolutely clear, and makes the point repeatedly, that the liberation of the blacks in the South is inseparable from the liberation of the whites. Faulkner's work makes all too separately clear that liberation cannot simply limit itself to allowing the black man to accede to the position of the white man—that position must be transformed. However, that transformation is never addressed directly by Faulkner and, partly as a result of this, Snead's argument comes close to a pessimism that would see some form of discrimination (not necessarily based on race) as inevitable, the ineluctable accompaniment of the will to power as knowledge.

This pessimism is completely set aside in the current book. Produced under the impact of a black history and a current black struggle, *White Screens, Black Images* is shot through with anger and with hope. The book demonstrates how central the representation and exclusion of blacks has been to the most powerful of twentieth century art forms. But it also celebrates the growing power of a black cinema which is determined to challenge those representations and exclusions. At the same time, and this might have been the missing conclusion of the book which would have engaged with Lee's films, there is no consideration of the paradoxes of representation which were sketched so forcefully in the Faulkner book. The current struggle over representation in the cinema is not linked to the struggle of representation itself, the Utopian question as to whether the repressions necessary to make a world exist can be decoupled from central repressions which would anchor this world in sexual and racial difference.

It might be tempting, if one did not know James, to read the move from European modernism to Faulkner to black cinema as a growing acceptance of blackness of the kind that Stuart Hall has recorded so forcefully in his accounts of his own intellectual development. But James Snead was of a younger generation to Stuart Hall and had been reared on the slogan of "I'm black and I'm proud". I myself would therefore read this movement in a slightly different manner. James was, and was conscious of being, the first generation of his race to be raised in the purple of the white educational establishment. He was determined to conduct his intellectual life at the most strenuous level, engaging with the most difficult and central arguments about representation. His development follows his growing belief that those central arguments inevitably involved questions of race. Unhappily he was prevented from following this development to their full conclusion. Whether he would have been able to link the political positions of *White Screens/Black Images* to the profound philosophical pessimism of the Faulkner analysis and to have engaged both across the full range of his experience is a question that is impossible to answer.

What is certain is that this book is in and of itself a major contribution to film theory. In the last decade much of the most serious work in film theory and history has been concerned with very local analysis. The overweening ambitions of the early seventies when the semiotic analysis of Metz was linked to Althusserian Marxism and a Lacanian psychoanalysis to produce a general theory of film has given ground to much more precise formal analyses and much more specific film history. There are many positive elements to these developments—it is no exaggeration to say that much of the early theoretical work made assumptions which were entirely based upon ignorance and that our understanding of the multiple determinants of any particular film is now vastly improved. At the same time there is a risk that this correction has in its turn gone too far and that we risk losing sight of the crucial role that film has played in the forming of twentieth century attitudes and values.

White Screens/Black Images redresses this balance. The analysis of particular films and histories is at the service of a general attempt to understand how film dramatizes and enacts fundamental social divisions.

Snead understands "film as (in the words of Jean-Luc Comolli and Jean Narboni) "ideology presenting itself to itself, talking to itself, learning about itself". My work on Hollywood film analyzes film stereotypes in terms of codes they form, and makes these codes legible, inspecting their inner workings, as well as the external historical subjects they would conceal." (p. 2) By stressing how codes mobilize a whole series of expectations Snead is able to break out of an analysis which simply analyzes representation of blacks in terms of positive or negative images. It is through the deployment of the notion of code together with the associated concepts of "marking" (the fact that blackness is always over-emphasized) and "omission" that Snead is able to demonstrate how central the representation of blacks is to Hollywood's overall vision of the world.

One of the great merits of Snead's book is that it reminds us how historical analysis must be informed by contemporary filmmaking and, at the same time, how our understanding of contemporary film is immeasurably improved if we understand its historical context. Snead's reading of the classic Hollywood tradition enables him to stress the importance of the work of contemporary black filmmakers in Britain and America. At the same time his understanding of that tradition grows out of his real engagement with that contemporary work. What James Snead discovered in film was a field in which historical analysis could feed into contemporary practice. I have no doubt that Snead's work will have important consequences for film theory but those consequences will feed back into both black and white filmmaking as Snead's analyses sharpen our perception of what is at stake in the representation of race.

There could be no more fitting memorial.

Pittsburgh, September 1992

Foreword

Cornel West

A New Kind of Intellectual

I first met James at a lecture by Jacques Derrida at Yale. He was then an assistant professor of Comparative Literature at Yale; I, an associate professor of Philosophy of Religion at the Yale Divinity School. We talked for hours: about the relation of deconstruction to certain forms of Greek skepticism, Herman Melville's conception of American racism as set forth in *Benito Cereno,* the relative silence of black critics regarding the work of James Baldwin, the new wave of black divas in opera, the emergence of rap music. We did not say one word about film.

Despite our intense schedules as young black intellectuals in a white academy, we managed to spend some time in dialogue about once every other month, always highlighting what we had read recently and how our vocations as intellectuals were changing. For example, we often talked about recent work done on Nietzsche. Or I'd give him a report about my lunch with Derrida to which I inquired about Derrida's African and Jewish origins and to what degree he considered himself a "third world" intellectual. And though we were always in a hurry, we'd find time to listen briefly to some new jazz he had bought— jazz that I rarely knew of. James was one of the first multicontextual and transnational intellectuals of African descent whose commitment to the life of the mind was absolute. We both were deeply committed to the idea that nothing human was alien to us, and that a decolonized mind entailed pursuing an examined life that critically embraced the best of our black traditions that helped sustain us, the best of European modernity that challenged us, and most importantly, the best of our unique, culturally hybrid selves so that we could create something new and novel in the world of ideas and, maybe, in the lives of other people, especially black people. In short, we wanted to fashion a distinct style of being an intellectual, a profoundly black style continuous with yet singularly different from earlier styles. This black style refused to view itself as *solely* black yet it recognized that without our New World African dimensions, our intellectual contributions—in European languages and with Euro-American training—would be diminished.

Indeed, James Snead represents a new kind of black intellectual in America. Unlike those of old, he felt no need to "prove" his intellect and worth. He also had overcome any inferiority anxieties regarding the authority of "white" recognition. With secure black family roots in New York (including a mastery of jazz and classical piano), a superb record of academic achievement at Exeter Academy and Yale College, a Ph.D. from Cambridge University, a few years in Germany, where he worked in a bank, and yearly trips to Egypt, Turkey and the Middle East, James was a true New World cosmopolitan of African descent.

James was fascinated with Africa, especially Egypt. His yearly trips to Cairo seemed to set him on fire, exciting with new perspectives on how we understand and conceive of "the West." Some of these insights may be found in his huge unpublished novel entitled *Cairo*. In fact, I suspect that much of who and what James was can be found in his large corpus of fiction, a corpus I knew little about when he was alive. In short, Africa seems to have been a crucial source of his profound intellectual engagement with the West.

And it is precisely the quality of James's intellectual imagination and the dogged determination to engage the West critically that enabled him to be such a superb critic of literature and film. His fine book on Faulkner speaks for itself, as do the sections on Thomas Mann and James Joyce he excluded from the book. His essay "Repetition as a Figure in Black Culture," reprinted in *Out There: Marginalization and Contemporary Cultures* (MIT Press, 1991), co-edited by Russell Ferguson, Trinh T. Minh-ha, Martha Gever and myself is a classic work in American and Afro-American letters. His journalistic treatments of James Baldwin's work are some of the best in this genre. And this present text, which is what we have of his projected book on black images in Hollywood films is, I believe, in a class of its own: something far beyond historical reportage, journalistic impressionism, narrow political seeking out of positive or negative black images, or ahistorical theoretical treatments of "blackness" distinct from specific black bodies and concrete black practices. Shunning parochial perspectives that ghettoize black films, James examines the array of black images shot through the Hollywood film industry, from *King Kong* to *Guess Who's Coming to Dinner* to the early moments of contemporary black film. Like Toni Morrison's groundbreaking work of literary criticism, *Playing in the Dark*, James's film criticism examines the variety of black images in the classic American film tradition and in the classic black film tradition, as well as the overlap of the two.

This examination requires a theoretical framework that highlights more than the obvious political aspects of black filmic images. It also entails a subtle psychocultural inquiry into the sexual dynamics of black filmic images, dynamics neither separable from nor reducible to racial politics and filmic form. James's book is one of the first efforts to engage upon this delicate terrain in a sustained way. As Colin MacCabe rightly notes, the soil tilled by James will bear much fruit in those critics yet to come.

The death of James Snead robbed America of a great mind and loving spirit, a young, gifted and black theorist of tremendous talent who was full of life and laughter. No critic concerned with race in film studies—quite different than black film studies—has yet produced such sophisticated and subtle readings of cinematic representations anywhere near those found in the best of *White Screens, Black Images*. The scope of James's interests, the breadth of his knowledge and the quality of his mind remain unmatched by present-day film critics concerned with black image on white screens.

How I wish James were around to make sense of the recent renascence of black filmmakers and the contemporary preoccupation with black images—as in *Deep Cover* and *The Crying Game*—by nonblack film makers. There is no doubt that Spike Lee, Reginald and Warren Hudlin, Julie Dash, Isaac Julien, John Singleton, John Nkumfra, Charles Burnett, Marlon Riggs and other black filmmakers are transforming the way black images are constructed and received. Similarly, talented critics such as Armond White, Coco Fusco, bell hooks, Michael Dyson, Michele Wallace, Lisa Jones, Nelson George, Greg Tate, Valerie Smith and, especially, Wahneema Lubiano are helping us understand aesthetic value, social weight and political relevance of these new filmic practices. To this new generation of artists and critics I recommend James Snead as exemplary of the highest achievements of black intellectual work and life.

1

Spectatorship and Capture in *King Kong*: The Guilty Look

In the mid-seventies, film studies witnessed an increased awareness of the place of blacks in the history of American films. A rich and generally informative series of books appeared around the overall subject of "the black image in films." Among these were Edward Mapp's *Blacks in American Films* (1972), Donald Bogle's *Toms, Coons, Mulattoes, Mammies, and Bucks: An Interpretive History of Blacks in American Films* (1973), James P. Murray's *To Find an Image* (1973), Gary Null's *Black Hollywood: The Negro in Motion Pictures* (1975), Daniel Leab's *From Sambo to Superspade: The Black Experience in Motion Pictures* (1975), and Thomas Cripps's *Slow Fade to Black* (1977). These studies all, in various ways, stressed the need for more positive roles, types, and portrayals, while pointing out the intractable presence of "negative stereotypes" in the film industry's depiction of blacks. While the thoroughness of such books was welcome, their clustered appearance contributed to an unfortunate homogeneity. For the mid-seventies were also the period of a most productive ferment in film theory, one which the above-mentioned books on blacks in film either uniformly ignored, or of which they were unaware. Invaluable semiotic, poststructuralist, feminist, and psychoanalytic tools were neglected, and still have not been adequately applied to the large body of Hollywood films in which blacks appear. The "black Hollywood" books of the seventies took a binary approach, sociological in its position, hunting down either "negative" or "positive" images. Such a method could not grasp what closer rhetorical and discursive analysis of racial imagery can. Few of these books investigate the filmic text or its implied audience. When black images and spectatorship are the issues, then such an approach seems indispensable.

I submit that this is part of a larger project, one that understands film as (in the words of Jean-Luc Comolli and Jean Narboni) "ideology presenting itself to itself, talking to itself, learning about itself."[1] My work on Hollywood film analyzes film stereotypes in terms of *codes* they form, and makes these codes legible, inspecting their inner workings, as well as the external historical subjects they would conceal. My term "code" is informed by the usage developed by Umberto Eco in *A Theory of Semiotics:* roughly, a set of conventions defining perception in limited and predictable ways within any given culture. Roland Barthes, particularly in his *S/Z,* conceives of an allied concept of codes, one related to the social and artistic conventions and rituals of everyday life. There are, according to Barthes, three major categories of narrative codes: codes which involve conventions of plot content (code of enigma and action); codes involving the structure of the plot (symbolic codes); and codes that the text borrows from outside sources (cultural or semic codes), or what we might call "stereotypes."

I shall outline a general conceptual framework and then move to a discussion of a well-known Hollywood film, *King Kong.*

My work on Hollywood films has to do with broad issues of power, domination, and subordination as represented in visual media, but I shall be concentrating here mainly on Hollywood's perceptions of blacks. In other words, much of what I say here might apply to other non-white groups that filmmakers have depicted in their stories: American Indians, Spanish Americans, Asians, and so on. But I agree with W.E.B. DuBois, when he said that the "Negro" is the metaphor of the 20th Century, the major figure in which these power relationships of master/slave, civilized/primitive, enlightened/backward, good/evil, have been embodied in the American subconscious.

From the very first films, black skin on screen became a complex code for various things, depending on the social self-conception and positioning of the viewer; it could as easily connote white superiority and self-regard as black inferiority. The message of black inferiority, however, was addressed to viewers who desired a sense of clear-cut dominance within the often confusing uncertainties of American history. Historical ambiguity requires some sense of transhistorical certainty, and so blacks were as if ready-made for the task. Onscreen and off, the history that Western culture has made typically denies blacks and black skin of historical reference, except as former slaves or savages.

One of the prime codes surrounding blacks on screen, then—one much at variance with the narrative codes that mandate potential mobility for other screen characters—is an almost metaphysical stasis. The black—particularly the black woman—is seen as eternal, unchanging, unchangeable. (Recall Faulkner's appendix to *The Sound and the Fury:* "They endured.") The code of stasis arises in order to justify blacks' continuing economic disadvantage. Throughout the history of Hollywood cinema, in films from King Vidor's 1929 *Hallelujah!* through Steven Spielberg's 1985 *The Color Purple,* blacks' character is sealed off from the history into which whites have trapped them. The notorious "Africa" films have as their main function to reinforce the code of the "eternal" or "static" black. From *Tarzan, the Ape Man* (1932) right through such recent efforts as *The Jewel of the Nile* (1985) blacks in Africa are seen to behave with the same ineptitude and shiftlessness, even before the three hundred years of slavery and oppression, that they exhibited, according to Hollywood films, years later in America. The only explanation can be an enduring "black nature" that no historical tragedy or intervention has ever or could ever have been responsible for.

In such examples and others, one may formulate the history of black film stereotypes as the history of the denial of history in favor of an artificially constructed mythology about unchanging black "character" or "nature." The problem is that, especially in film, stereotypes and codes insulate themselves from historical change, or actual counter-examples in the real world. Caricatures breed more caricatures, or metamorphose into others, but remain in place.

Although films are not necessarily myths, as is sometimes asserted, certain films have managed to remain repeatedly compelling and thus

3

to assume a permanent, quasi-mythic status in a society's consciousness. The tireless popularity of such films might be related to Claude Lévi-Strauss's notion of myths as narratives that endure because they resolve—by venting latent social contradictions—conflicts that otherwise would remain troublesome.[2]

Yet poststructuralism has somewhat revised Lévi-Strauss's contentions, and the difference is crucial for understanding Hollywood stereotyping of blacks. For whereas Lévi-Strauss sees myths as *unifying* communities by giving concentrated and vicarious form to contradictions that plague them, I would suggest that modern myths precisely illustrate social *divisions,* exposing audience fantasies that are anything but communally shared. In a pluralistic society, myths—especially where they rely on the subordination of particular groups in society—are inevitably political and cannot enforce or sustain a uniform scheme of mythic reconciliation.

The three most frequent devices whereby blacks have been consigned to minor significance on screen include what I refer to as : *mythification; marking;* and *omission.*

Mythification involves the realization that filmic codes describe an *interrelationship* between images. American films do not merely feature this or that debased black image or this or that glorified white hero in isolation, but rather they correlate these images in a larger scheme of semiotic valuation. For the viewer, the pleasure of recognizing this ranking displaces the necessity of verifying its moral or actual validity.

Mythification is the replacement of history with a surrogate ideology of elevation or demotion along a scale of human value. Mythification also implies identification, and requires a pool of spectators ready to accept and identify themselves with film's tailor-made versions of reality. This device engages audiences on the level of their racial allegiance, social background, and self-image. Film translates the personal into the communal so quickly that elevation of the dominant and the degradation of the subordinate are simultaneous and corporate. When we consider *The Birth of a Nation* or *Gone With the Wind,* for example, the mechanisms of racial mythification are clear—the dominant "I" needs the coded "other" to function: white female stars (themselves coded as subordinate to white males) employ black maids to make them seem

4

more authoritatively womanly; white male stars need black butlers or sidekicks to make them seem more authoritatively manly. Soon, by mythification and repetition, white and black filmed images become large-scale models, positive or negative, for behavior, describing (in the manner of myth in non-Western societies) structures, limits, and an overall repertoire from which both white and black viewers in the real world select possibilities of action and thought.

The second tactic is *marking*. As if the blackness of black skin itself were not enough, we seem to find the color black repeatedly overdetermined, marked redundantly, almost as if to force the viewer to register the image's difference from white images. Marking makes it visually clear that black skin is a "natural" condition turned into a "man-made" sign. Initially because of the shortcomings of early lenses and film stocks, but later due purely to the needs of image-making rhetoric—black skin has been over-marked in order to eliminate ambiguity. (In his article for the Fall 1985 edition of *Daedalus*, Brian Winston argues that from Edison through the present day, film stocks were designed to show off white skin to greatest advantage, but have never conveyed other skin tones with any degree of verisimilitude or subtlety.[3])

Marking is necessary because the *reality* of blackness or of being "colored" cannot always, either in films or in real life, be determined. The racial terms "black" and "white" refer to a wide range of hues that cannot be positively described—by being this or that—but only by negative contrast: black is not "white" (where "white" itself is a term difficult to fix). In early films, white actors used blackface, but even when black actors and actresses played black roles, studios required them to darken their skins (Bert Williams, Lena Horne, Nina Mae McKinney, and Fredi Washington are only a few examples of black stars who had to be so marked). The Hollywood black had to be made either very black or very light. In the movies *Pinky* (1949), and the second version of *Imitation of Life* (1959), the roles of mulatto black women passing for white are actually played by white actresses, to make sure that a visual ambiguity does not compound an already difficult conceptual leap.

Film is a medium of contrasts in light, and so the shades of skin color between black and white often must be suppressed, so that binary visual opposites might serve cinematographic as well as political purposes. Chauffers, domestics, porters, jazz musicians, and other blacks are marked by the black/white codings in the contrast between their skins and white articles of clothing. Aprons, gloves, dresses, scarves, headbands, and even white teeth and eyes are all signifiers of a certain coding of race in Hollywood films that audiences soon came to recognize. This is not to say that whites on film would not bulge out eyes, or wear servants' clothes; only that 1) blacks seemed to do it exclusively; and, 2) these signifiers have a different coding when whites are associated with them—indeed, this is what makes looking at them so interesting. White gloves, for instance, on a white butler spell "reserve, efficiency, and service," whereas on a black butler, they might contribute to an overall connotation of "racial inferiority." A white with an apron on might mean: "poor/lazy/unfortunate person—could end up either on the high or the low end of society, depending on the outcome of the film (role *not* connected to color)." A black with an apron on might mean: "they're so good with food/ children/animals—will remain in that position forever (role indistinguishable from color)." Other common markings include "Negro dialect" (early title cards in silent films even felt constrained to write dialect when blacks were seen to speak!); elevation/lowness; motion/ stasis; cleanliness/dirtiness; distinction/group-mass. All these *semes*, or smallest units of meaning, combine to form larger codes, like letters combining into words.

The third device is *omission*, or exclusion by reversal, distortion, or some other form of censorship. Omission and exclusion are perhaps the most widespread tactics of racial stereotyping but are also the most difficult to prove because their manifestation is precisely absence itself. The repetition of black absence from locations of autonomy and importance creates the presence of the idea that blacks belong in positions of obscurity and dependence. From the earliest days of film, omission was the method of choice in designing mass images of blacks. For example, the film of Jack Johnson's victory over his white opponent Tommy Burns (1908) was banned because of feared inflammatory effects. Typically in the thirties and forties, filmmakers would relegate their black stars to optional numbers that were edited out for Southern distribution. In general, filmscripts edited out the reality of blacks as lawyers, teachers, and doctors, in favor of far more arcane and restrictive black stereotypes. Even within the individual frame, we often (though not always) find the black excluded, peripheral, distant from the source and focal point of action. But since "framing," "editing," and "cutting out" are indeed the exigencies of filmic and aesthetic practice, it was possible to hide ideologically motivated distortions under the mask of artistic economy or exigency.

Against this general background, then, I would like to move on to a discussion of a film most of you know, *King Kong. King Kong* provides an especially telling example of the use of the devices of mythification, marking, and omission because of its blatant linkage of the idea of the black with that of the monster. "Monstrousness" is a complex dimension of Hollywood film, and for our purposes I will mention here the work of only one of the more incisive critics to have written about it, Robin Wood. Basing his insights on Marcuse's notion of "surplus repression," Wood has argued that contemporary society, repressing sexual desires that would otherwise threaten its stability, vents these desires through the figure of the monster.[4] The Hollywood monster film allows, among other things, a safe outlet of such sexual desires in a surrogate form, and a vicarious experience—pleasurable and horrific—of the chaos that such a release would bring about in reality. More specifically, Wood states that society represses: 1) "sexual energy itself"; 2) "bisexuality" (which he defines as the arbitrary nature of social norms surrounding masculinity and femininity); and 3) "female sexuality/creativity." A too strictly practiced internal repression may end in external oppression—a generalized hostility directed against a societal "other," especially the "other" as women or non-Western peoples. Applying Wood's paradigm to *King Kong*—a monster movie about blackness which stretches all boundaries, temporal, spatial, and natural—we see that repression and oppression are inescapably bound one to the other. For while surplus repression is primarily sexual, we must remember that the oppression it spawns is largely political. (Indeed, it has been variously argued that some whites oppress blacks on the outside in order to repress elements of "blackness" inside.)[5]

7

In *all* Hollywood film portrayals of blacks, I am arguing here, the political is never far from the sexual, for it is both as a political and as a sexual threat that the black skin appears on screen. And nowhere is this more plainly to be seen than in *King Kong*. There are very few instances in the history of Hollywood cinema in which the color black has been writ so large and intruded so powerfully into the social plane of white normality. Blackness in motion is typically sensed as a threat on screen, and so black movement in film is usually restricted to highly bracketed and containable activities, such as sports or entertainment. *King Kong* is an exception to this rule: the attempt to contain Kong fails, and he makes off with not just any woman, but with a *white* woman. *King Kong*, then, is a noteworthy, though perhaps surprising, instance of "the coded black"—in this case, the carrier of blackness is not a human being, but an ape, but we shall see that the difference can easily be bridged.

In their August 1970 analysis of "John Ford's *Young Mr. Lincoln*," the editors of *Cahiers du cinéma* say that films often contain "constituent lacks" or "*structuring absences* . . . the unsaid included in the said and necessary to its constitution." These absences "have some connection with the sexual other scene, and that 'other scene' which is politics."[6] My reading of *King Kong* will attempt to supply some of these constitutive omissions. Through a reading of the subplots in *King Kong*, we can see that the film's political aspects are hidden by the emotive nature of the sexual plot's covert build-up and ambiguous release. *King Kong* is able to cloak and leave unresolved a potentially explosive allegory of racial and sexual exploitation by manipulating the codes whereby films typically portray romantic conflict and resolution.

Unraveling the relationship between the sexual and political plots in the film means tracing the surface plot, the political subplot, and tracing the transformations of audience perspective implied by each. Few products of the American cinema have made such a rapid and indelible impression as *King Kong*. From its first release in 1933, the film was immensely popular, and it helped RKO at least temporarily survive bankruptcy. In *King Kong*'s wake, the director/producer team of Ernest B. Schoedsack and Merian C. Cooper made two sequels,

Son of Kong (1933) and *Mighty Joe Young* (1949), and others have followed these. Kong, the center of attention, has joined that group of cultural reference-points and large-scale metaphors that includes Frankenstein, Moby-Dick, Santa Claus, and Sherlock Holmes—neither kin nor foreign, neither completely real nor completely fictitious. One can buy postcards of Kong scaling the Empire State Building (recently, an inflated facsimile of Kong was temporarily hung there), or buy bumper stickers stating that "King Kong died for your sins."

Kong has become a classic in large part because of his very "humanness." As we shall see, the ape's "humanness" engages, but also conceals, the underlying political point the film illustrates. Early on in the production, there was some debate over just how human Kong should appear. The chief technician and animator, Willis O'Brien, wanted a sympathetic, anthropomorphic Kong, and won out over Cooper's more "monstrous" conception. In the end, O'Brien's artistic virtuosity helped "humanize" Kong, giving an eighteen-inch clay model familiar and often endearing gestures and expressions. The humanness of King Kong, the key to *King Kong*'s success, also tips us off to the various ways in which the film appeals to its spectators.

Plot Summary

The plot of *King Kong* is, as its makers continually stressed in interviews, absurd, very much like that of any typical adventure yarn. If we compare it with the plot of Melville's *Moby-Dick,* for instance, we find both similarities and differences: a somewhat obsessive leader and his crew journey into unknown seas without their full knowledge of his intentions. The group encounters a terrifying, murderous creature of fantastic dimensions. Yet here Carl Denham returns to New York with King Kong and even lives to make an oration over his corpse, while neither Ahab nor his men (except for Ishmael) returns from the encounter with the whale. Another variation is the presence of Ann Darrow (her name almost certainly alludes to Clarence Darrow, defense lawyer in the 1925 Scopes "monkey" trial), usually referred to simply as "the girl"—in most cases, such seafaring adventure tales

9

are womanless. These two peculiarities—the importation of the monster into civilized society, and the addition of a woman to the adventure model—are quite pertinent. The film has four main divisions: 1) New York and the discovery of the girl; 2) the voyage; 3) encounter with natives and Kong in the primeval jungle; 4) New York and the death of Kong.

The first shots of the film place us in New York Harbor, seen from Hoboken, and the various docks, ships, and cargoes suggest "trade," "commerce," and "transportation." As in *Moby-Dick*, we hear about the expedition's leader before we see him. Carl Denham (Robert Armstrong) is a theatrical producer, ruthless in his pursuit of "pictures," even under the most dangerous circumstances. He has chartered a ship called the "Venture" and its hold, curiously, is full of explosives and gas bombs. Denham wants to get underway, but he has not found what he needs most for his film: "The public, bless 'em, must have a pretty face to look at. . . ." The aggressive Denham searches Depression breadlines for the right woman. In the Bowery he sees Ann Darrow (Fay Wray) reaching for an apple from a fruitstand. The proprietor berates her, but Denham "rescues" her by paying for the fruit. The girl is well-bred, and has some acting experience, so Denham promises her "the thrill of a lifetime" if she will come with him, and assures her that he has no improper interest in her. Haltingly, she agrees to sail with crew.

The second part takes place as the ship is underway. Ann seems to be enjoying the trip more than the first mate, Jack Driscoll (Bruce Cabot), who is openly hostile to women. In their first encounter, he slaps her accidentally. He apologizes to her, but insists that she does not belong on such a dangerous mission: "Women just can't help being a bother." As time goes by, however, their relationship warms. Meanwhile, Denham has told Driscoll and Captain Englehorn (Frank Reicher) about an island west of Sumatra, in uncharted waters, where he has heard there is a huge wall, "built so long ago the people who live there now have slipped back, forgotten the higher civilization that built it." The wall is there to keep something out, "something neither beast nor man . . . monstrous, all-powerful, still living, still holding

10

that island in a grip of deadly fear . . . I tell you there's something on that island that no white man has ever seen . . . if it's there, you bet I'll photograph it." He gives Ann Darrow a screen test on the shipdeck, coaching her to react in fear to an invisible assailant.

In part three, the ship reaches what they now call "Skull Island." Through the dense fog, the crew hears the sound of drums. At daybreak, a party lands on the island, and sees the wall: ". . . it might almost be Egyptian . . . Who do you suppose could have built it?" Denham exclaims: "What a chance! What a picture!" Soon, they see a group of blacks dancing in a rite that seems to center around a young girl with garlands around her neck. Denham shouts out: "Holy mackrel! What a show!" Ann shouts: "I want to see," and pushes forward from the protective men around her. Denham says "If I could only get a picture of that before they see us. . . ." Soon the Chief (Noble Johnson) stops the dancing. The witchdoctor (Steve Clemento) has complained that the Americans' presence has spoiled the ceremony. The Captain, who by chance knows their dialect, tries to placate the Chief, who is now demanding Ann as the sacrificial object, to be exchanged for six black women. To this offer, Denham says "Yeah, blondes are pretty scarce around here," and signals a slow retreat to the boats.

Ann and Jack declare their love for each other that night: "I'm scared for you"—Jack says—"I sort of guess I'm scared of you, too." Reluctantly, they kiss. Soon afterwards, two blacks abduct Ann from the ship. Jack, discovering her absence, organizes a rescue party armed with guns. Meanwhile, the blacks have substituted Ann for the girl in the rite. Now decked with garlands, Ann has been strapped to a high altar beyond the wall and abandoned there. Watching from the wall's ramparts and gates, the Chief hits a giant gong, invoking Kong, who approaches the stone columns to which Ann has been tied. She screams, in earnest now, as Kong takes her into the primeval jungle.

The rescue party forces its way past the gates into a realm of prehistoric creatures. Denham says: "If I could only bring back one of these alive." Some of his men are eaten by a plesiosaurus, others fall into a deep ravine as Kong shakes them off a tree trunk they have

1. *King Kong.* A monster movie about blackness.

been using as a bridge. Soon Kong is taking Ann up to his cliffside lair. Jack follows him there, arranging that Denham should return to the ship for help.

Jack, by lucky timing, rescues Ann from Kong's dwelling. They swim back to the beach, pursued by Kong, who devastates the village in his wake. Denham shouts "We came here to get a moving picture, and we've found something worth more than all the movies in the world. . . . If we can capture him alive." Finally, Denham is able to immobilize the ape with gas bombs. He stands over the fallen ape's hulk and says "Why the whole world will pay to see this . . . We'll give him more than chains. He's always beenking of his world, but we'll teach him fear . . . We're millionaires, boys."

In the fourth part, Denham is seen backstage at a Broadway theater

2. *King Kong.* Kong and Ann (Fay Wray): the look.

with Ann and Jack, telling reporters about the "eighth wonder of the world" he is about to unveil. He tells the first-night audience: "I'm going to show you the greatest thing your eyes have ever beheld. He was king and a god in the world he knew. But now he comes to civilization, merely a captive, a show, to gratify your curiosity . . ." The curtain rises, and the terrified crowd sees Kong standing on a huge platform, restrained by a halter around his neck and chained to steel crossbars by the wrists.

Denham tells the photographers to take the first pictures of Kong in captivity, but as the flashbulbs go off, Kong stirs, thinking they are harming Ann. He breaks free and searches New York for Ann, causing death and havoc. He finds her in an upper-story hotel room and takes her from Jack while he is still unconscious. Perhaps mistaking it for a tree, he climbs the Empire State Building with Ann in his hand. Jack suggests that the police try to shoot him down. Kong, now at the top of the building, puts Ann on a ledge and fights off the planes, but in vain. Six fighters attack him repeatedly with machine guns, he

3. *King Kong.* The chained Kong on theatrical display.

4. *King Kong.* The Empire State finale.

falls off the building and dies. Jack climbs to embrace Ann while Denham stands over the fallen ape's corpse delivering the final lines: "It wasn't the airplanes. It was beauty killed the beast."

Supplying the Omitted Plots

One of the more interesting aspects of this synopsis is that it betrays immediately the contradictions and instabilities of the presumably "happy" ending. Whose story is it? Certainly for Ann Darrow the narrative ends happily: she has gone from a solitary Bowery existence to her lover's arms atop the Empire State Building, and has achieved no small degree of fame in the process. Similarly, the lure of beauty has taken Jack from the sea and promised him a blissful domesticity. But in the end, the relationship between Ann and Jack survives only at the cost of an execution. The narrative pleasure of seeing the (white) male-female bond re-established at the end tends to screen out the full meaning of the final shot: the accidental (black) intruder lies bloody and dead on the ground, his epitaph given glibly by the very person who has trapped him. Kong's plot has the least happy ending of all. As we shall see in D.W. Griffith's *The Birth of a Nation* (1915), a desired political end (the erasure of the black/savage from white/civilized society) has been represented in a plot that gives it a justification that seems necessary for narrative reasons (the reconciliation of the white marriage unit). For whose sins, then, did King Kong die?

The story of King Kong becomes comprehensible only if we replace what has been left unsaid, and refuse to be diverted by the familiar mechanics of the "love plot." It is no accident that Denham is the keenest proponent of the "love angle" on the events he has brought about. From the beginning, he has explained Ann's presence by the need for there to be a "beauty" if there is to be a "beast," and at every juncture until Kong's death, he underlines the "beauty and the beast" notion. His interpretation is supported by the opening titles, with their relation of "an Arab proverb" which claims that once the beast disarms himself in the face of beauty, he is as good as dead. The opening moments of the film, then, predispose the spectator to accept Denham's platitudinous reading of the film. But, as we learn during the

15

film, Denham is anything but a reliable and disinterested commentator. An alternative reading would suggest that the film is not about Jack and Ann, or about Kong's actions, but really more about the motives and effects of Carl Denham's deeds—all the more so, since he is the only character who remains unchanged from beginning to the end, and is throughout the tale the driving force behind the plot's events. What, then, is the deeper nature of his "venture"?

On a purely film historical level, we could call *King Kong* an autobiographical, self-referential film, and not be too far from the mark. Cooper and Schoedsack met under trying circumstances in a foreign country, and seemed bent on repeating that initial experience on film. Their early film careers took them on dangerous expeditions to bring back, not animal skins or precious artifacts, but pictures of exotic subjects. Their joint ventures *Grass* (1925) and *Chang* (1927), filmed respectively in Iran and Thailand, still count as milestones in the ethnographic film tradition. While *Grass,* almost in spite of its makers' efforts, ended up as a more or less straight ethnographical document, in *Chang,* Cooper and Schoedsack manage to integrate a preconceived plot with location shooting (to the detriment of the film's ethnographic value).[7] While on another expedition in Africa, they came up with the idea of a film involving many of the elements of *King Kong,* although their first idea was—incredibly—to make the film in Africa without the use of any special photography. Many incidents in the film, including the "discovery" of Ann Darrow in the Bowery, were based on actual events. According to one source, Cooper told the scriptwriter, Ruth Schoedsack (his collaborator's wife): "Put *us* in it . . . Give it the spirit of a real Cooper-Schoedsack expedition."[8] Moreover, Cooper and Schoedsack used the same secrecy and tantalizing advertising about *King Kong* the film that the fictional Denham uses to promote King Kong, "the eighth wonder of the world," and the creature also makes a rather striking debut on the stage of a large Broadway theater. In fact, one of Cooper's publicity gambits involved placing large cannons at the entrances to the theaters where *King Kong* was showing, with placards reading "this theater is armed to defy King Kong." Possibly then, Denham's coup fulfills the imaginary desire of the Cooper-Schoedsack type of moviemaker, and also the imaginary fear of

16

the horror movie audience: instead of bringing back pictures, Denham brings back the real thing.

Plot One: Blackness Captured

On a more deeply historical level, we discern the first stage of what I called earlier "the political plot." Let us rewrite the plot in the form of a question: what happens when an entrepreneur engages on a "venture" to capture certain views of what he calls a "lower" civilization? Denham's adventure resembles any one of a number of forays by Europeans to non-European nations in search of animals, minerals, artifacts, photographs—and even human beings. The moral of the tale might concern what happens when "savages" are brought back into "civilization" for profit. Recall that although at the beginning of the film, Denham's explicit purpose is only to take pictures, it is not long until he begins to think of taking things, and soon after, he gets what he wants, as a merely natural continuation of visual forms of capture. A sort of *optical colonization* precedes and prepares for an actual one. *King Kong* cleverly distorts the metaphorical connection between Denham's journey and the European-American trade in African slaves by setting the story in the Pacific, "west of Sumatra," and yet portraying the islanders not as Malays, but as "Oceanic Negroids."[9] As an allegory of the slave trade, then, and of various other forms of exploitation and despoilment, Denham's journey might be expected to resemble what we already know about Europe's encounters with traditional (and in this case, African) peoples.

The ambitions of the "Venture"'s crew and leader evoke ideals at the heart of the West's economic success and psychological self-esteem. The ship, as we learn in the first few minutes, is leaving with dangerous "cargo" (dynamite, guns, and bombs), and will likely return with tamed "cargo" (in the event, black cargo). This transaction is the very definition of "trade," and no less of the slave trade. Hence, Denham's expedition, eccentric on the surface, is intimately linked (as in the establishing shots of New York harbor) with the centers of world trade, and the very authority of American commerce and enterprise. He has an inherent right to go to other cultures and interfere in their

17

affairs, as long as his plans work out. He is just trying to make an honest return on his backers' venture capital.

The assumption about the white male's "other"—other races, women—is that they will remain passive means to Denham's ends. The venturers make a clear separation between "lower cultures" and "higher cultures," and jump to the racist conclusion that the island's great wall could not possibly have been built by "the [black] people who live there." Despite their sense of separateness from the "native" population, the "Venture" crew enlists its aid when it is expedient (when, for example, Kong storms the walls looking for Ann): "Good work!," Captain Englehorn shouts at the blacks. Yet the arrogance of the crew towards these "ethnics," then, is more than just a reprehensible attitude. Historically (in slavery and colonialism) as in this film, such attitudes culminate in the often successful attempt to humble, humiliate, or even annihilate the victim. Recall Denham's words just after Kong has succumbed to the gas grenades: "He's always been the king of his world, but we'll teach him fear." Reading Kong as a captive, Denham's pleasure in showing Kong off on a stage platform (in every sense, an "auction block") takes on a certain historical pungency.

Women, similarly to blacks, appear not as people or potential partners, but as objects of others' stares, a sort of visual capital. Remember that, despite Ann's early fears, Carl Denham's interest in her is not even remotely sexual. In fact, his contempt for women in the film is only matched by Jack Driscoll's. The non-sexual, homocentric impulses of the leading men, left unchecked, will eventually destroy the fabric of society as certainly as King Kong would destroy its exterior. Carl is obsessed with money, is orally aggressive and visually avaricious (greedy for things to see and photograph); Jack mistrusts women and desires solitude or at best all-male companionship. Carl's interest in Ann is purely economic, not personal—her blonde hair, blue eyes, and fair skin qualify her for his preconceived "beauty and the beast" scenario. Soon, one sees that the misogyny of the males (Jack and Carl Denham) threatens the continuance of a potential white marital bond more surely than King Kong's infatuation with Ann.

The visual design of the film itself encourages a strict separation and hierarchy of blacks and whites: the black "natives" receive the kind of cinematic *marking* of "jungle blacks" that we have seen elsewhere, and which films like *King Kong* and *Tarzan, the Ape Man* (made the year before) helped to canonize. We already know what can be expected from the Skull Islanders, as they are coded in advance for their later demise. Blacks' function here is literally that of "props" (derived from "stage properties"): figuratively owned by the whites' appropriating "look"; soon to be literally owned through various modes of exploitation. They are well "directed" in the film, and provide the "jungle film"—no less than the grass huts or the wall or the palm trees—with its indispensible and unchanging background. The first marking is an auditory one: drums. Since the "Venture"'s crew arrives at the island in fog, they actually *hear* the island and its blacks before they *see* it. *King Kong*'s score (composed by Max Steiner) is a virtual handbook for aural coding, managing to convey in Wagnerian-style leitmotifs the semantics of particular scenes. Cooper was not exaggerating when he claimed that as much as a quarter of the film's overall effectiveness came from Steiner's music. The creature's horrific growlings and the orchestral climaxes vie with each other in trying to convey in sound the extreme transgressions of normality on the screen. Steiner's coding of blackness by "the drum" founds (in the relatively youthful art of synchronized movie sound) a longstanding cinematic device—though it was seldom used as subtly as it is here.

Later, we see the blacks in their ritual dance. For a 1933 screen audience, black skin was a code for limited narrative range. Blackness in such a context could not but mean "the primitive," "the elemental," as well as "the marginal," the "unproductive." So the blackness of the South Pacific islanders serves a semiotic function, introducing us, as it were, to the most primitive human beings before we later encounter the most primitive flora and fauna (foremost of these fauna, Kong himself!). The islanders' facial paint, shields, spears, headdresses, and lack of clothing are physical markings that restrict their potential for narrative action: we suspect that, like Kong, they are futureless: they will either disappear and perish or be forced to serve or entertain those who have "rescued" them.

19

The filmic marking of the islanders as small-scale surrogates for Kong—whose mass seems to have absorbed the conglomerate blackness of his worshippers—becomes even clearer when one notes that some of the blacks in the ritual have made themselves up in Kong-like skins. In Western culture, the literary and historical tendency to identify blacks with ape-like creatures is quite clear and has been well-documented. A willed misreading of Linnaean classification and Darwinian evolution helped buttress an older European conception (tracing from as early as the 16th Century) that blacks and apes, kindred denizens of the "jungle," are phylogenetically closer and sexually more compatible than blacks and whites: "the Negro-ape connection served as a sufficiently indirect means by which the white man could express his dim awareness of the sexual animal within himself."[10] Merian Cooper's actual words to Fay Wray take on a new meaning against this background. She asked him for some information about who her leading man in his new project (Cooper was being, much like Carl Denham, quite secretive) would be. Cooper could only promise her that she would be playing opposite "the tallest, darkest leading man in Hollywood."[11] Indeed, in the film, Carl Denham's description of Kong as "neither beast nor man" might serve as a racist's description of the black person.

In light of the issues discussed above, one might read *King Kong* as a way of dealing with the question: what is the worst that can happen, now that the monster-savage has come into civilization? America, in the midst of the Great Depression in the early thirties, was already undergoing profound traumas, and several have suggested that King Kong's rampage through the streets of Manhattan "served to release the pent-up anger and frustration and fear of the millions who had been pitched headlong into the Great Depression . . . a rampaging gorilla . . . scales [the] bastion of capitalism, the Empire State Building."[12] There were racial, as well as economic tensions in the North, however. Black migration from the South to the North doubled between 1920 and 1930 as compared to the previous decade. The race riots of the early twenties (many of them in the North) still hovered in the collective memory, their recurrence an ever-present possibility. In divergent but equally insistent ways, the Harlem Renaissance and the first Scottsboro trial (1931) kept the unsolved question of race at the forefront of white attention, even as whites often attempted to ignore the presence of the black. So for audiences in 1933, and presumably ever since, the image of an amorous black ape running amok in New York City with a white woman he has abducted must indeed have addressed on some profound level the question of how to deal with the "cargo" that the twin imperatives of trade and greed have caused to be imported from the non-Western world.

Plot Two: Endangered Women

A second and related political plot involves the use of the figure of the woman as a justification for various kinds of subterfuge and violence. As we have seen, *King Kong* diverges from typical adventure plots both by including a woman on the voyage and by bringing the monster back. Both variations allow related ideological propositions to be advanced. Ann Darrow ("the girl") has more in common with King Kong than it seems at first. If Kong is objectified blackness ("beastliness" in the white aesthetic), then the girl is objectified beauty—both are "freed" from a lowly state, but must then "serve" Denham's design. They only exist to satisfy the male viewer's active and erotic look. Denham's wish to see what "no white man has ever seen" testifies to a peculiar sort of cross-racial voyeurism, ostensibly shared by the spectator he serves, particularly given the way in which he plans to excite the black-ape by teasing his appetites with the "bait" of the girl (the film's German title of the film, *King Kong und die weisse Frau,* "King Kong and the White Woman," conveys what is at stake with greater explicitness than the English). Just as Kong and the natives are coded for their blackness ("primitiveness," "earthiness"), the woman is "coded for strong visual impact so that [she] can be said to connote *to-be-looked-at-ness.*"[13] For Denham, the value of the beast and the girl lies only in their juxtaposition, a combination based upon pre-existing sexual and visual conventions in Western iconography— a positioning that for most of the film threatens to destroy the girl, and that does (as the opening titles already reveal) finally annihilate Kong.

21

But the coding of Ann's body goes even further. She is not just "beauty," but also "endangered beauty." Freud might locate a certain sado-masochistic nucleus in Denham's desire to see the "girl" molested or at least scared out of her wits by a black ape representing remorseless phallic potency. But these drives are not confined to Denham's case: instances of the endangered woman pervade the history of Hollywood film. The agents threatening the woman are often, if not always, black, then coded as representatives of darkness. If the covert result of endangered beauty is to furnish the spectator with a certain illicit titillation, the overt result, as here, is to elicit the attention—and usually, the violent retribution—of the white male. Only a violent abduction of the girl by two blacks (small-scale surrogates for Kong, who later abducts her himself) can shock Jack out of his male-centered fancies and into an active concern for the heterosexual bond.

The girl has several other functions on this particular voyage. As we have seen, the film uses her as the center of erotic energy, thereby diverting both visual and intellectual attention from the purposes of Denham's trip. For the audience at least, she offers a secondary rationalization for Denham's theft of Kong. The reasoning would be: the blacks (and later, Kong) have stolen the girl, and therefore Denham is justified in stealing Kong (and anything else he wants to take) in return. True to form, Denham does not even use this justification, because he sees the removal of Kong not as theft, but as a good business proposition. In any case, the viewer's attention focuses on the danger that the girl seems to be in, while overlooking the actual dangers to which Kong (blacks) is being exposed. As opposed to the graphic display of the blacks' acts of theft, the film's discourse completely ignores the "removal" of Kong to New York. The film leaves out, as it were, the entire slave trade, the voyage, and the 200 years of slavery in the New World. It goes straight from the African "discovery" to the American "insurrection."

The silencing of the plots sketched out above takes place on the level of filmic diegesis. One simply refuses to notice these concerns, swept along by the techniques of smooth closure and suture at which film practice had, by 1933, become very adept.[14]

Plot Transformations: Spreading the Guilt

I would like to outline three ways in which the political plots are transformed, and suggest why these transformations are so effective. The first transformation, as we have seen, subsumes all sense of political reality beneath the "love plot." The second engages the spectator in a series of fantasized visual exchanges which loosen the initially heavily coded oppositions of black/white, female/male, savage/civilized, beast/human. This temporary suspension of racial and sexual fixity only makes them seem even more necessary once the viewer returns to more ordinary reality. The third transformation makes the narrative of Denham's conquests into a story about *seeing,* and thereby draws us into a necessary complicity with its imperatives.

The rhetorical problem of the monster film is to elicit the spectator's guilty participation in a number of normally repressed fantasies, and to project the viewer's sense of guilt onto the otherness that the monster represents. The manipulation of the spectator occurs through the usage of the coding measures outlined above, but at key moments, film also manipulates point-of-view as a way of suggesting identifications that will have an ideological effect later. Part of the pleasure of the cinema, after all, is the sense it gives us of spatial ubiquity and authority (a sense that Lacan, at least, would term "imaginary"). At times, as in a novel, the spectator is placed in the film by an omniscient point-of-view, at times by a character, at times by both, and at times steps completely out of the filmic point-of-view (the spectator then realizes he or she is in a theater, watching a film). The spectator's place "is a construction of the text which is ultimately the product of the narrator's disposition towards the tale."[15] It is not true that we identify only with those in a film whose race or sex we share. Rather, the filmic space is subversive in allowing an almost polymorphically perverse oscillation between possible roles, creating a radically broadened freedom of identification. But this freedom only increases the guilt that comes from looking at that which should remain hidden.

For the white male viewer, the forceful and successful Carl Denham and perhaps even the "love interest" Jack Driscoll are obvious locations of identification. Black male viewers might identify in an alienated way with Denham's authority, experiencing their identification with his authority almost as a compensation for their submission in real life to similar authorities. Women viewers might not find Ann as "ideal" a "model" as Denham does. Her sniffling timidity and incessant screaming grate on one's sensibilities, yet they are only extreme versions of behavioral codes that here and elsewhere connote female weakness. The weakness of the female, as we have seen, provides the chance for males to test and confirm the range of their strength.

Ann's terror, if not her reactions to her terror, is believable enough. Through her, white male and female viewers experience fear and passivity vicariously, although for a black spectator, her position—being terrorized by blackness—could only be shared with the greatest psychic conflict.

If Robin Wood's paradigm is correct, then the figure of King Kong would allow the white male to vent a variety of repressed sexual fantasies: the hidden desire of seeing himself as an omnipotent, phallic black male; the desire to abduct the white woman; or the combined fantasy: to abduct a white woman in the disguise of a phallic black male. Barthes suggests that bourgeois society's initial response to otherness is either to ignore it, to deny it, or to assimilate its privileges and trappings, albeit at a safe distance.[16] But that assimilation of otherness, particularly if it releases repressed desires, is brief, and comes at the cost of increased guilt, a guilt that is often discharged in the oppression of the other. Kong's ultimate punishment (public execution by firing squad) seems an expression of this dynamic. The ending, then, would have different effects on different viewers. A white male viewer might sense in Kong's death a cleansing of his previous identification with the beast. A black viewer might not only reject the price Kong pays for his own "guilt," but also would wonder why there is no price to be paid by Kong's exploiters.

As we have seen, there is a tenderness about the ape, which would imply that it has absorbed all aspects of otherness: not only the black male, but also the female. The black spectator, while free to assume any position in the film, would need to contain temporarily a wrenching ambivalence about its white-centered discourse—one that connects exclusionary or debasing signifieds to the black's chief signifier of skin color—since it is from this discourse that the narrative pleasures of the film derive. Identifying with Kong would bring similar pleasures to black audiences as to white viewers, but it would be less easy for a black viewer, in most cases, to shrug off Kong's demise and death and to replace it with the image of the happily unified white couple.

The camera's visual rhetoric facilitates an almost promiscuous violation of social roles and limits: monster/human; woman/male; savage/civilized; black/white. By various exchanges of glances, looks, and camera angles, a space of mixed identity soon arises, exchanging and connecting our (here, the camera's) "look" with the viewpoints of normally discrete subjects. For example, the film tends to pose threats to the girl from the left-hand side of the frame, with the girl on the right. And the film's (as well as the publicity posters') basic black-white confrontations involve blackness threatening whites from the left: the first landing; Ann's kidnapping from the boat; King Kong's first approach to her on the sacrificial altar. Yet during the screen test on the boat, whites threaten Ann in the same way: Denham, on the left, photographs Ann, on the right. The series of shots that follows (close-up of Denham; Ann sends a mock scream in the direction of Denham's camera, and us) exactly anticipates the sequence that occurs when Kong later approaches her (close-up of Kong; Ann sends a real scream in Kong's direction). Rather than providing us in both cases with a distanced spectatorial set-up, the camera shuttles us between subjective points-of-view, even those of the monster: Denham's, and Kong's. The ubiquitous camera has no scruples, it seems, about class, race, or even species: the *need to see* is more important, as the film progresses, than the *need to separate* or the *need to repress.*

There is one telling exception to this rule: the camera never assumes the subjective point-of-view of the blacks on the island (although a "third-person" view reports certain events that the white crew cannot have witnessed). Given their absurd behavior and witless manner, identification with them would require an emotional generosity that most white spectators simply could not muster (perhaps a few black spectators would be able to separate the actual black actors from the degraded roles they assume).

Perhaps the most difficult transformation to resist is our gradual implication in Denham's optical colonialism. Even a viewer repulsed by Denham's many negative qualities would have difficulty escaping the pull of his powerful voyeurism, or the way in which his obsessive need to look at spectacles—to see things immobilized on stage or on screen—imposes upon its objects not a neutral mechanical process, but a deleterious form of framing. The "capture," applicable to photography as well as the hunt, well expresses the dual aspect of framing otherness. The political ideology of the film soon becomes inextricable from the pleasure we take in the very act of seeing. The power of staging a "show" (watching a "girl" scream or "natives" dancing) is no longer Denham's alone. *King Kong,* by a rather devious movement, makes us cheer him on. Indeed, Denham frequently justifies his most ruthless wants by calling them ours: "the public, bless 'em, must have a pretty face to look at. . . ."

The ideology that the public represents would only be able to use blacks and women as something singing, dancing, or otherwise "to be looked at." We never question Denham's right to "pick up" the girl, or to interrupt and photograph the island rite, or to abduct Kong, because it is precisely the act of photographing that defines his (and our) feeling of mastery over what we see. And only through photography have we been able to satisfy our own "need-to-see." Yet it becomes clear that for Denham, the line between importing a "show" and importing a "captive" has blurred. Recall that he introduces Kong to the New York audience as "merely a captive, a show, to gratify your curiosity." His usage of the same word, "show," for his first sight of the blacks' ritual recalls the slavery plot again: "Holy mackerel, what a show!" Black captivity is not far away.

Denham not only transforms the political plot into a plot of seeing, but he also continually changes his own definition of what seeing entails. At the beginning, he claims that he only needs a picture of "beauty," but in fact he does not photograph Ann but takes her (as he later takes Kong) into his physical possession. In a sense he has already reached his stated goal at the start of the plot: he can have both the picture of "beauty" and the real thing (Ann) herself without even leaving New York. But what he really wants (although he does not say this) is the girl's *meaning* as an ideological *code*. His picture

26

must show her *in danger,* thus eliciting a display of "manly" protectiveness and supporting the connection between "female weakness" and "male strength." So Denham needs a photograph of the girl being threatened by King Kong. In this sense, Kong is both a part of his goal and a potential pitfall for his design.

In the event, Kong not only threatens Ann, but abducts her as well, seeming to undermine the quest for the perfect film, but in fact hastening its production. For Kong's actual abduction of the girl incites the male response better than a mere picture could. It also brings the threat itself into Denham's physical possession: now he has not only got his pictures, but he has at least two subjects—the girl and Kong—that others will pay to see and photograph, especially as a pair. Denham's obsession with seeing licenses unlimited ventures, but it can never be satiated, particularly in its specific form as the wish to see (and later possess) what "no white man has even seen."

The momentum of the plot transforms the viewer's question "what will Carl Denham's venture exploit or destroy next?" into the question "what will I see next?," a question that seems more harmless than the first one until one considers the close linkage between seeing, capturing, and killing that Denham's actions and the film establish. The photographers that Denham invites to Kong's "showing" threaten to restart the "seeing-capturing" cycle, and so it is no accident that at this point, Kong intervenes to stop the vicious visual cycles.

"An ethnographic film may be regarded as any film which seeks to reveal one society to another" but *King Kong,* however unflatteringly, is an ethnographic film that reveals one society to itself, or perhaps more exactly, reveals to its spectators the diversity and ambivalence of spectatorship.[17] *King Kong* teaches us that the viewer's need for spectacle and vicarious enjoyment may issue from deeper needs, ones that many people are willing to pay, steal, and even kill in order to satisfy. Denham, although his obsession is particular, would stage fantasies about generally repressed sexual, political, and historical violations. Hence, King Kong dies for everyone's sins, not just for Denham's. The general guilt inheres in the general gaze.

2

The *Kong* Sequels

The "Kong" sequels are obsessed with Denham's (and his *Mighty Joe Young* variant, Max O'Hara's) guilt about prior actions. *Son of Kong* (1933) was a hasty and largely unsuccessful attempt to capitalize on the success of *King Kong*. *Mighty Joe Young* (1949) revises the circular plot of *King Kong*—it starts out in Africa, and gives the ape a happy "back-to-Africa" ending ("Joe" is taken from Africa to America for profit, but this time he returns alive, as arranged by a now-contrite O'Hara). The same animation team, under Willis O'Brien, produced similar spectacular effects in both sequels, but the central figure and the central situation in both were not equal to their originals.

There are some peculiarities of both films that deserve mention. In *Son of Kong*, for example, there is never any real reason to assume that the ape at the center of this film (smaller and younger than King Kong) really is Kong's "son." This attribution comes from a Denham who seems inclined to project his guilt about Kong onto the first giant primate he sees. The movie is obsessed with the killing of King Kong: in the first shot of the film, the camera dollies back from a promotional poster of King Kong, tacked to the wall of a now-destitute Denham who is hiding out in a New York City rooming house to escape his creditors. Denham begins the film not only in guilt, but also in *debt*—to those whose property King Kong has wrecked, and more remotely to King Kong and his descendants (at one point, he says "I know it sounds funny, but . . . I felt I owed his family something"). Early on, he addresses the poster on his wall, in answer to a reporter's question: "Don't you suppose I'm sorry for the harm he did? I wish I'd left him on his island. Old Kong, I'm sure paying for what I did to you." So dual debts—financial and moral, to society and to King Kong's "survivors"—must be paid, and, characteristically, Denham uses old tricks to attain his ends: he embarks on another risky seagoing venture.

Returning to Skull Island, this time in search of buried treasure, Denham faces the same temptations to exploit as before, except that this time, there is no camera: the capital sought here is purely physical, and not visual. We get the same Steiner music when the "natives" appear. They seem as angry at Denham as the New York debtors are, as relayed by Captain Englehorn: ". . . his village is destroyed and his people are killed, and it's all our fault for leading Kong inside the walls." The job of repairing the damage done in *King Kong* will be complex, and *Son of Kong,* unfortunately, makes the diminutive "son" carry the entire weight of Denham's atonement to the father.

Denham seems repentant throughout the scenes in which Kong's son appears. At one point, Captain Englehorn asks Denham "you really feel conscience-stricken about Kong, don't you?" Later, Denham and the "girl" (this time, a singer who stows away on Denham's ship) notice that the ape has cut his finger. The girl feels "sorry for him," and Denham bandages the finger, addressing the son, as follows:

You're not a patch on your old man. I must be completely cuckoo doin' this: giving you a first-aid treatment instead of running like blazes. It must be remorse or something. You see, I'm the guy that knocked out your pop with a gas bomb and then carried him off to New York in chains. I've been sorry for it ever since . . . well I guess if I'd left him alone, we'd all have been better off . . . This is sort of an apology.

Despite this apology, Denham uses Kong's son to retrieve the hidden jewels for him—he screams, characteristically, "We're rich!" Finally, King Kong's son dies, saving Denham and the girl from an earthquake

5. *Son of Kong.* Blackness diluted and domesticated.

during which the entire island sinks into the sea (presumably drowning all the natives, too).

It is clear that the plot is being asked to carry too much symbolic weight here; the narrative runs off into confused, yet highly revealing, directions. Even as Kong's son is made to receive the apologies of Denham, the price of that atonement is his self-sacrifice for Denham. The ape's services to Denham late in the film compensate for the treachery of a group of whites defined as the "other" earlier in the film—namely, Captain Englehorn's crew, which has mutinied and sent the "bosses . . . where all captains belong, over the side" in a single rowboat, with which they eventually reach Skull Island. The contemporary political overtones of this confrontation (when they approach Denham with their grievances, he says "We must be in Russia: here comes a committee of the workers"), unique among the three "Kong" films, might have something to do with a certain sentimental preference in the thirties for what was considered "faithful" black labor, seen as potentially less dangerous than the unruliness of agitated white

Northern working classes. It is not impossible that the film is suggesting that if the Northern white entrepreneur of the thirties would only atone for the "harm" of American racial history, he might have a more obedient and loyal labor pool than the white Northern labor force, demanding equality, would provide.

The somewhat paternalistic attitude of Denham and the girl towards this "baby Kong" (who, interestingly, is *whiter* than his progenitor, fitted out with greyish hair, which makes him seem either quite old or quite young, but at any rate, no longer the monolithic symbol of potent and threatening blackness that King Kong had been) is incompatible with the overriding assumption of the film, which is that we are to consider the "Son of Kong" to be at least as menacing or frightening as his father. In this film, there are times when "baby Kong" seems to provide the Denham-girl couple with its symboic (un-)natural offspring: harmless, "cute," even adoptable. Blackness has been diluted and domesticated here, and the film loses the entire vortex of psychosexual energy that motivated its predecessor. Whereas King Kong seemed at times the very embodiment of Freud's "id," the "son" seems to have nullified the id in order to come to the white couple's aid. The underlying message may well be that, even if white sins may be acknowledged, there is no question but that Denham's aspirations will be supported at the expense of the black "other." If King Kong died unwillingly for Denham's sin of avarice in the first film, then here King Kong's "son" sacrifices himself willingly, almost as if to "thank" him for his contrite attitude. Only in this way can Denham profit once more without sinning again.

Mighty Joe Young makes explicit *Son of Kong*'s implicit "adoption" configuration. In this film, the "girl" has bartered for a baby ape and raised it from cradle to giant. Here, as in *King Kong*, the monstrous ape (power under the control of beauty and sentiment) and its white female shadow are transported to America (Los Angeles this time, reflecting actual shifts in the scene and focus of American entertainment between 1933 and 1949), lured once more by a sleazy entrepreneur, Max O'Hara (played by a now older Robert Armstrong). The final of the "Kong" trilogy merges aspects of the other two—most strikingly, here we have both the crime and remorse: O'Hara first cons the girl and the ape into leaving Africa, and later, after Mighty Joe Young goes berserk and destroys his nightclub, spends the latter part of the film helping Mighty Joe Young evade execution by the authorities. At one point, he sounds the "remorse" theme again: " . . . listen honey, I've been doing a lot of thinking: if Joe gets shot, it's my fault . . . I talked you into this, and it's up to me to get you out. I'll get you back home, if I have to go to jail for it . . ."

The "Africa" from which Mighty Joe Young springs is scarcely distinguishable from the fake "Africa" that O'Hara creates for his "theme" nightclub in L.A. The opening credits are followed with establishing shots of what is presumably supposed to be East Africa— a superimposed title says "AFRICA," in case we miss the point. But immediately the picture rings false: the white father and daughter (the mother has died) living on an African plantation are surrounded by African "natives" who are dressed in Indian, rather than African garb, and who, amazingly, don't speak even pidgin English! The whites, of course, seem to speak the local tongue—usually in the imperative voice—especially the young "Jill," who barters with the Africans, disarming them with her charm, getting them to sell her the little ape, whom she names "Joe."

The Los Angeles club, called the "Golden Safari," features black doormen dressed as "natives" (the same actors as in the "Africa" sequences, though they are presumably playing American blacks playing Africans). The dance numbers, like those as we shall see, in the early club scenes of *Blond Venus* (1933), are a strange amalgam of Amerindian, South Pacific, and African iconography. The curtain is modeled after the containing fence on Skull Island. Here, the overall conceit of the "Kong" series is made manifest: reintroducing the trappings, and even the representatives, of barbarity into civilization, albeit in a "defanged" form. Even the Skull Island natives had used King Kong in this way, "staging" his periodic appearance and propitiation behind their containing fence "curtain," regulating his performance by their elaborate rites and human sacrifices. The "natives" were to King Kong as the "Golden Safari" audience is to the real Mighty Joe Young as the movie audience is to the movies *King Kong* and *Mighty Joe Young* themselves. This film, like *King Kong,* is partly about its own perfor-

6. *Mighty Joe Young.* Black muscle supports and saves effete white culture and its agents.

mance: staging a spectacle for a fickle and anxious audience, in which mythic contests of gigantic proportions are underway (recall the test of strength in which Denham pits Mighty Joe Young against the "ten strongest [white] men" from all the white races in the world: "Is there one creature in all the world powerful enough to overcome that combination?," he asks—yes, is the answer, and he is *black!*). The climax in both films, also, comes in a moment where the spectacle is disrupted by the violent abdication of the monstrous black actor, causing panic and chaos. It may be true that "Joe wouldn't hurt anybody; he won't if you treat him right," as Jill argues, but white spectators in these films are invariably cruel, and monstrous black difference is inevitably mistreated.

Mighty Joe Young's debut in the "Golden Safari" comes with him lifting up Jill and her baroque grand piano (she is playing "Beautiful Dreamer," Joe's favorite song!)—a suitable image of the "beauty and the beast" parable that has run throughout the Kong trilogy: black muscle supports and saves effete white culture and its agents. Yet eventually, predictably, blackness disarmed becomes blackness exploited, and O'Hara and the audience takes turns humiliating the ape and, indirectly, his keeper. Despite these impositions, however, Joe is able to acquit himself as King Kong never was. Not only Max O'Hara (in saving Mighty Joe Young from the firing squad), but also Mighty Joe Young (in saving the children from the burning orphanage) are able to perform their good deeds in this picture, leaving no ethical loose ends by the end.

Joe began and ends the film as a child substitute for Jill, who once accommodated him in her own former baby cradle, but obviously, there must eventually be a father to complete this bizarre family unit. By the end, Jill does have a companion, Greg Johnson, cowboy, previously called "Lasso Lance" whose preference for women is considerably more marked than was the case with Jack Driscoll in *King Kong,* finally settles down with Jill—and Mighty Joe Young—in Africa (he told her early on in the film that she seems "at home" in Africa). This film's happy ending, then, comes without the physical sacrifice of the agent—Joe—who in effect brought the couple together, yet this does not mean that it ends without certain subtle kinds of compromise.

The film ends with O'Hara watching a film of Jill, Greg Johnson (the male lead), and Joe, with O'Hara giving us an explicitly formulaic voice-over—"And they lived happily ever after . . . they're back home, where they belong." Of course, there is never any doubt that the white couple "belong" in Africa as obviously as their adopted black, semi-human "child," Joe. In any case, *Mighty Joe Young* actualizes an implicit, but failed, inclination of *King Kong*—to humanize, assimilate, and domesticate black "otherness" (Joe's body, unlike that of Kong's son, is very black indeed), except that here, the film takes the further step, essential to colonialism: "domestication" now means making Africa over into our "home" rather than making the African other "at home" in America. Mighty Joe Young (who was the mightiest thing outside of Africa) is returned to Africa only on the condition that Africa (consider Rhodesia or South Africa) be made into a place where whites can now "belong" as masters of all they surveyed, including the no longer "mighty" Joe Young.

The Kong trilogy remains a perhaps unequaled dissection of the various layers and strains of Western racial and sexual fantasy, and serves up a perhaps endless menu of contradictions, compromises, and subterfuges, all in service of what the films of the thirties did best: the glorification and mythification of archetypal white male and female types, and the canonization of their typically lopsided alliances. The need to isolate tabooed drives under the cover of blackness ended up creating a perhaps unwanted effect: the taboo- (and often property-) smashing black became less a figure of reproach or repudiation than a pitied and even admirable surrogate fantasy. Whereas the initial purpose of these films may have been to demonize blackness, further dividing the "normal" white citizenry from its carriers, the actual effect may have been to glorify the strength and doggedness with which these exploited creatures fended off attacks from a hostile white society. King Kong may have died for our sins, but his life continues to give the form of our drives a local habitation and a name. Realizing that they had created an immortal figure of blackness, and an allegory of American race relations, Cooper and Schoedsack, to their credit, carried the conceit over the course of three films even further than their society could: through plunder, exploitation, and humiliation to guilt, reparation, and finally, repatriation.

3

Birth of a Nation

One of the more useful products of Christian Metz's well-known theory of film semiotics lies in the distinction he attempts to make between "cinematic" and "extra-cinematic" codes. In society, the code rarely is the same as the message, and one of the tasks of the semiological analysis attempted in my study is to move centrifugally from the films' explicit messages to their underlying codes and to the mythologies (borrowing Barthes's term) which clusters of these codes ultimately support. In *Birth of a Nation* (1915), for example, the assumption that Elsie Stoneman, or any daughter, will break off her relationship with her sweetheart Ben Cameron at the father's request is an extra-cinematic code, found in Dixon's novel as well in the social text of the last century. The message is that "Elsie decides to leave Ben at her father's request," but the code suggests that here, as in all such circumstances, society expects that "the father's will must be done." Griffith incorporates this extra-cinematic notion of "loyalty to the father" into the film, articulating it through various shots that, in the course of telling the story, we accept as cinematic codes to be recognized and registered on each subsequent repetition. For the sake of their narrative momentum, we tend to leave unexamined the extra-cinematic codes they represent. The Cameron's black maid (played by a white actress—in Griffith's film, *marking* of the color black is achieved by often implausible expedients), in her white apron and cap signifies the message "here is a uniformed housekeeper," but the underlying code is "blacks are customary as servants; black is the natural color of servility." As Metz suggests:

> Between 1911 and 1915, Griffith made a whole series of films having, more or less consciously, the value of experimental probings, and *Birth of a Nation*, released in 1915, appears as the crowning work, the sum and the public demonstration of investigations that, however naive they must have been, were nonetheless systematic and fundamental. Thus, it was in a single motion picture that the cinema became narrative and took over some of the attributes of a language.[1]

In general throughout the history of coding the color black in mainstream American films, it is precisely the intentional confusion of narrative, cinematic, and extra-cinematic codes that tends to undermine the color black on screen. Roland Barthes calls these "referential codes"—references to a generally accepted notion of "common sense" or the established knowledge of the time: they enable all manner of extra-cinematic ideologies to hide under accustomed codes of narrative closure.

Birth of a Nation does not merely represent the beginning of many cinematic codes, found here for the first time in any film, but also represents the culmination, refinement, and further dissemination of certain extra-cinematic codes concerning blacks and whites. Here as elsewhere in the over seventy years of film history since Griffith, film language serves, above all, the telling of a story. As Metz suggests, "*it was precisely to the extent that the cinema confronted the problems of narration* that, in the course of successive groupings, it came to produce a body of specific signifying procedures."[2] Yet the principal mechanism of cinematic racism—certainly in the films we are considering here—is precisely to sublimate itself under the stronger compulsions of romance, revenge, or sensation that belong to the allure of film narrative. We are, as a rule, more interested in how things come out for the dominant relationships in the film than we are in dissecting the racist codes and assumptions either imported from the extra-cinematic world, or manufactured within the film itself. In unprecedented ways, film form and racism coalesce into myth here, seemingly myths of entertainment but ultimately ones political in nature, ones that continue to assert their presence today. The powerfully signifying procedure of film language, invented at the service of narration, are at best morally ambiguous and at worst (as in the case of Griffith's title cards, for instance) blatantly tendentious. It is perhaps no accident that, while we owe Griffith the early encoding of cinematic devices like close-ups, pans, tracking-shots, parallel montage, and other ways of signifying successivity, precession, temporal breaks, causality, adversary relationships, spatial relationships, and so on, we also find these narrative figures facilitating our acceptance of the virulence of the extra-cinematic codes—existing in the real world prior to *The Birth of a Nation*—which might be called their raw material.

The plot of *The Birth of a Nation* is quite simple, structurally. The first part encompasses the "Civil War" and the second part might be called the "race and revenge" plot, culminating in the forging of an alliance between Southern whites (Ben Cameron's "Ku Klux Klan"), "good-hearted" Northerners (such as Elsie Stoneman), and "loyal" black servants, all emblems of the harmonious bonds of this newborn nation. Throughout both parts, there are various "courtship plots" which are the true center of the spectator's interest, and which are resolved at the same time as the "race and revenge" plot. It is interesting to note that the scene-by-scene rhythm of the film almost compulsively alternates the "courtship plots" with the others. In the first part, love alternates with war; in the second part, love alternates with revenge against the black usurpers. The effect is to rivet our interest in a favorable romantic outcome while treating the political parts of the plot as mere trifling obstacles to ultimate consummation between Ben Cameron and Elsie Stoneman. The balance in this oscillation is never lost; one almost supposes that the Civil War and the black were invented to delay a "happy ending," or that solving the nation's intractable racial and economic problems is as easy as two people falling in love.

The film's movement from order to chaos and back to restored order resembles the structure typically found in horror or disaster movies, and by all measures, one must call blackness, in all its shades, the dark nightmare at the center of this disaster fantasy, one which

7. *The Birth of a Nation.* Elsie Stoneman (Lillian Gish) marches with the Klan.

must be removed for order to be restored. Yet the paramount claim of Griffith's film is precisely that it is not a collective anxiety dream, but that it is archival, a mere filmic record of events that happened not too long before. Thomas Dixon's 1905 novel, *The Clansman* (later made into a play), certainly intended to re-write history, asserting both that things were better when blacks were docilely upholding the plantation economy, and yet that the nation would be better off without the specter of their presence. Griffith's film, to the extent that it is full of wonderful visual detail, can only compound its precursor's confusions. One title card claims that the "Old South" was a time of idyllic wonder, "a way of life that never would be again," but another, coming within seconds of the first, asserts that "the bringing of the African to America planted the first seed of disunion," and that a unified nation could only be born after the black man, restored to his place, gave up all pretensions at equality. This is the basic ideological message of the film: some blacks can be loyal retainers, more devoted to whites than to themselves, but they must universally be barred from intercourse, of any kind, with white purity.[3]

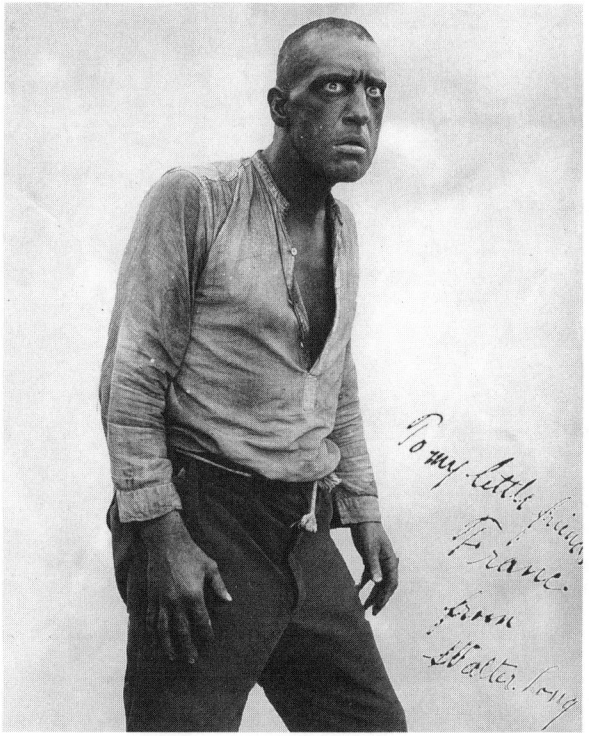

8. *The Birth of a Nation.* Gus (Walter Long), "a renegade negro." The white actor as black villain.

The term "history" is not casual here. Even if one does not find concrete evidence that U.S. President and erstwhile Princeton historian Woodrow Wilson actually said after a private White House screening of *The Birth of a Nation* "It's like writing history with lightning!.," it is still a self-conscious aim of *The Birth of a Nation* to write history with cinema, particularly with its so-called "historical facsimiles," which are both obtrusive and dilatory to the plot, but which are crucial to ideological, rather than narrative, aims. These "facsimiles" include: "Lincoln conscripting 75,000 volunteers"; "The Confederate surrender at Appomattox"; "Lincoln's assassination at Ford's Theatre"; "The Negro Party in control in the State House of Representatives"; "Historic incidents from the first legislative session under Reconstruction." The film seems to procrastinate, delaying its love and revenge plots

9. *The Birth of a Nation.* "The Negro Party in control in the State House of Representatives."

for a moment, to say "and not only is this fictional story compelling, but the historical facts are true as well."

Of course, the enterprise of selecting out a particular moment of history to serve as "origin" or "birth" is never completely free of the possibility of distortion. Most ask neither "what breed of 'nation' is being born here, with the violent founding of the KKK?" nor "what happened to the previous 300 years of American history?" As we have seen, one of the earliest paradoxes in the title-card narrative occurs when we read: "the bringing of the African to America planted the first seed of disunion." Never mind the absence of the enslaving subject here (*who* brought "the African . . ."?), and the complete obfuscation of the motives and greed at the center of the slave trade. By this simple phrase, years of crimes and unsavory motives are effaced. Even on the surface, though, the title-card narrative clashes with the visual evidence. The shots of blacks in cotton fields and the close-up of the cotton boll shown soon after this title card themselves return us to the "seed" metaphor. While blacks happily picking cotton seeds in the fields are represented as the pride of a lost Golden Age (their labor being the "seed" of wealth which made antebellum Southern aristocratic life in Piedmont, South Carolina, or anywhere, possible), they themselves are being called the "seed of disunion." Somehow, they cannot be both. The overarching irony of the film is implicit in the contradictions of the film's opening moments, but effectively disguised by the momentum of narrative: the "seeds of disunion" were not the blacks who picked the cotton, but literally the cotton seeds themselves. Griffith's close-up reveals the "seeds" of discord, even as he displaces the guilt from the white cotton planters to the black hands that reap the cotton. The widespread avarice and lust for wealth, leading to a labor-intensive agricultural economy that was both comfortable and insupportable, ultimately set North against South. Blacks, innocent bystanders and victims of this system, become, by mere visual juxtaposition, the convenient repositories of blame for its fated collapse. It is as if Griffith's visual narrative here displays the contradictions of Dixon's written narrative to which it is trying to be faithful: the image tells us that cotton was to blame, but the title cards blame the bringing of the "African to America." The "Birth," then—a title chosen only at the last minute to replace *The Clansman*—becomes a moment of false origination, false "birth," for America, one that is well belated; the film allows a complete erasure of the slave trade, the economic motives behind it, and the suffering it unleashed; America is "born" in the 1880s. The first thing that must be said of Griffith's "history," then, is that, even on its own terms, it has a confused sense of history.

But part of the purpose of Griffith's film is precisely to reproduce "nostalgia" as "history," rather than to advance plot. The establishing shots of blacks dancing in the slave quarters, or picking cotton in the fields are more akin to the novelistic statement "here is the way it was" than "here's what happened next." They, though not labeled "historical facsimiles," are similarly designed to give a "documentary" view of "the way things were" in a time and place that most of the audience could not have known first-hand.

Siegfried Kracauer's opposition of the two basic "tendencies" of cinema—the "realistic" tendency (Lumière), and the "fantastic" tendency (Méliès)—is relevant here.[4] Simplistic as it may sound, one must never forget the apparently phenomenological "truth-value" of a medium that is in fact custom-made (to a greater extent than still photography) to produce true-seeming lies. Kracauer presupposes a constitutive delineation: some films use the medium to truthfully record what the camera sees; others deliberately use camera tricks to create an imaginary scene that never existed. Even those which combine the two tendencies must have a "balance between the realistic tendency and the formative tendency. . . ."[5] It is perhaps in the earliest stages of film that we notice this split in its most naive form, possibly chuckling nowadays at the rather obtrusive way in which Griffith's title cards intrude on the plot to tell us periodically: "you are watching the absolute truth . . . seeing is believing." Particularly the convention of claiming that his "facsimiles" were taken from actual eyewitness photographs (the State House of Representatives scene is "after a photograph by The Columbia State"), or accounts (the Appomattox surrender is rendered "after Col. Horace Porter in 'Campaigning with Grant'"), seems on retrospect Griffith's poignant attempt to pass off a false representation as a true "reconstruction," and to make us somehow forget the cinema's falsifying potential. Yet at the time of the film's release, and ever since, many seem to have been completely taken in. The merging of the "archival," the "ideological," and the "narrative" here becomes the seminal recipe for coding subsequent propaganda films.

So Griffith's "reconstruction" film also attempts its own kind of cinematic reconstruction, contradictory on the surface perhaps, but well hidden by the rapid and pleasing succession of images and title cards. Yet despite its vituperativeness against blacks, mulattoes, scalawags, carpetbaggers, and Northern troops, *The Birth of a Nation* is in fact a conciliatory film, and one of the more puzzling of its missions is both to castigate the behavior of some Northerners after the war, while at the same time offering a symbolic reunification of North and South (at the expense, it should be added, of black claims to justice).

It is perhaps the extreme tension between vituperation and glorification (often of different members of the same group) that exacerbates the already present extremes of racism in the film. Although many have complained about the one-dimensionality of the black images in *Birth of a Nation,* it must be said that the entire film hinges on a flimsy superstructure of scanty stereotypes, from the well-intentioned but misguided Austin Stoneman to his abolitionist comrades to his angelic daughter, to the cadaverous-looking, skeletal Lincoln himself, defined solely by whiskers and stovepipe hat (and the epithet "the Great Heart"). Recall that his "fostering hand" kindly helps the downtrodden South, with this Northerner even pardoning the falsely accused Confederate soldier, Ben Cameron (in a scene to be exactly borrowed two decades later in the Shirley Temple movie, *The Littlest Rebel*), at the request of his loving mother and the Congressman's daughter, Elsie Stoneman.

Throughout the film, in the manner of vaudeville and stylized theatrical conventions since the 18th Century, only the grossest physical differences (whether of skin color, gesture, or physiognomy) were used, in order to signify identity at a great distance in no uncertain terms. The entire characterization of the lovers, familial relationships, courting behavior, and rituals of honor derive from long-standing extra-cinematic codes which cannot be solely attributed to Griffith's racism. Finally, simplification and reduction to type are the motors of every narrative, and the only moral or artistic question that remains is one of degree. Yet most would agree that the distortions here are not piecemeal or gratuitous, but systematic and fully interwoven with the larger diegesis of the film.

A word about the title cards is appropriate here. They serve the typical function of the gap, the space, the hiatus in all sorts of discourse, providing that articulation that both interrupts and sustains the narration. Their impact here might best be termed "diacritical," since, as we have seen, their written message may have little or no concordance with the visual image on the screen, but merely, as it were, "interprets," or "slants" that image in a tendentious direction.

4

Shirley Temple

Shirley Temple, child-star extraordinaire (she received a special Academy Award at the age of six), particularly in her films with Bill ("Bojangles") Robinson, constitutes a significant reference-point for the mythification of the white female in the films of the thirties. It may seem strange to say this, given the singularly "adult" sexual appeal of Marlene Dietrich, Mae West, Bette Davis, and the like; Shirley Temple cuteness might seem to exclude her from any serious consideration in such company, but her precocity only hints at underlying transformational equations between seemingly different worlds in all her films. Mythification, we recall, is a process of glorification or magnification by contrast, and the comparatively grand stature that Shirley Temple attains in these movies is quite revealing about the nature of cinematic mythification in general, especially given her actual diminutiveness. Not only does she connect (and often reverse) the worlds of youth and adulthood, but also merges the codes of black and white on a sustained level that the screen has never seen before or since.

Shirley Temple characters signify a certain ability and license given to presumably weaker members of society (children, women, and even blacks) to transgress barriers of decorum and convention with virtual impunity. In the same way, paradoxically in the racist climate of the thirties, black maids (notably Hattie McDaniel) often surprised white theatergoers with their brashness and even presumption *vis-à-vis* their white masters. Similarly, the strongly mythologized white woman of thirties and forties movies often exploits the male's mythification of her to derive an incremental power not prepared for by what we know of contemporary gender relations. There is something selfish, unrepressed, and child-like about the film personae of Hollywood's *femmes fatales* of the thirties (we shall be discussing three of these—Mae West, Marlene Dietrich, and Bette Davis—in this section), a certain strength that comes through their seemingly instinctive manipulations and negations of white male society. The raw genius for this kind of violation gets its purest display in the pert characterizations created by Shirley Temple.

Shirley Temple's career began with short films in which she parodied the great female box office stars of her day. Her roles in Jack Hays's series called "Baby Burlesks" involved scenes in which babies reenacted adult situations. The word "baby" is not figurative; the parts were played, in the era before stringent child-actor laws, by children so young that the routines are now almost painful to watch—Shirley herself was not quite four. Later, in such films as *Stowaway* (1936), she continued to do impressions of such adult stars as Al Jolson and Ginger Rogers. So Shirley Temple's films are about almost everything else but childhood and children. Instead, they feature adults looking at themselves through the obverse mirror of childhood. Indeed, one could say that in all these films, Shirley is doing her most sustained impression—imitating not adults, but an adult's image of a child. As with many other "child-star" vehicles, their relevance can always be directly found in adult concerns, anxieties, and tensions. The explicit comic point is the humorous contrast between the overcontrolled adult paradigm and the hapless incompetence of the kids' reproduction. The deeper psychological effect, however, is that adults look at the innocence of the "baby burlesks" with an implicitly covetous eye.

Especially for white females of a certain class and rearing in America, society seems intent on asserting as positive values the habits, trappings, and mannerisms of extreme childhood that Shirley Temple emulated brilliantly: it is, even today, as if certain groups of women could aspire to no greater image or model than to have a squeaky voice; dimples; curls; feigned innocence; over-idealism (for a modern filmic example of this glorification of child-like attributes, see the roles of Shelley Duvall, or perhaps even more so, Diane Keaton's screen persona—particularly in *Annie Hall*). A kind of *Narrenfreiheit* ("fool's freedom"), which excuses in a child (or woman) a brashness otherwise punishable in an adult (or male), can also help recreate this model. With Shirley Temple, we find that her candor is excused as harmless, though we cannot but notice in these films that Shirley Temple is anything but harmless, being usually more canny and effective than the adults around her. She turns the condescensions and prejudices of the adult world against that world.

The genius of Shirley Temple characters lies in the way in which they have become disciplined negotiators between two opposing worlds—much like blacks, who have similarly been plunged into the role of children, amidst often hostile and at best patronizing white adults. If Shirley Temple's characters will presumably be allowed to grow out of their childhood, then perhaps much of the pathos of these films (particularly *The Little Colonel* and *The Littlest Rebel*) comes from knowing that her dancing partner, Bill Robinson, and his entire race—addressed by first names, or the word "boy"—are relegated to servile and dependent status and hence can never escape the imposition of a child-like mask that whites can don or discard at will.

In knowing the adult world better than adults themselves do, Shirley's characters manipulate their way into success and vindication. But even these acts of sassy subversion have a price. The deeper irony of the Shirley Temple persona is that her circumvention of white adult norms and standards takes place within a formal context conceived and cordoned off by the adults who have made the film, and, as we have suggested, ultimately support and confirm the final legitimacy of an adulthood renewed and made tolerable by the discovery and co-optation of "the child in all of us" through vicarious identification with Shirley's qualities.

Bill Robinson's presence in the most memorable Shirley Temple films allows us to watch this process re-enacted in the realm of race, rather than merely age: just as mature audiences converted Shirley's youthful cuteness into some unable ideal that was to mollify the rigors of adulthood, we see Shirley throughout her films borrowing Bill Robinson's blackness in a number of instances: from emulating his

10. *The Little Colonel.* Bill Robinson and Shirley Temple in the staircase tap dance routine.

various dances (notably the "staircase tap dance" routine, in *The Little Colonel*), to co-opting the blacks' baptismal ritual for her own purposes, to her actual and visually startling expropriation of blackness (by wading in mud with blacks in *The Little Colonel*) to actually blacking herself up with boot polish for disguise in *The Littlest Rebel.* It is a patent fact of such movies, then, that under certain societal norms, blackness and the state of being a child are conditions of relative powerlessness made to converge. But Shirley's subversions also point, despite the political context, to wider possibilities of protest against a stifling environment. The conceptual interpenetration of blackness and childhood works both for and against the racist content of the films themselves.

Shirley Temple's young shoulders had a formidable burden placed upon them, and her striking lack of success after 1940—once she was

11. *The Littlest Rebel.* Shirley Temple as the littlest blackface performer.

obviously never to be a child again—tells us that the scope of her usefulness as a symbol, like that of the blacks in her films, was strictly confined. Shirley's magic only worked under certain controlled circumstances, whose narrow delimitations may explain why the plots of her films range from the mawkish to the blatantly implausible. Yet to examine that burden is to unveil the implied racial and sexual tensions and desires that made Shirley Temple such an object of fixation for an entire generation of Americans.

It is important to recall that in one of her earliest movies, a short called *Kid 'n Africa* (1931), she plays a missionary in Africa trying to civilize the "cannibal" tots, played by anonymous black kids. She is on the verge of being roasted by an African chef (wearing, of course, an Escoffier cap!) when a nursling Tarzan saves her, and together they set up a toddler's colony in the African wilds. Once more, we have the equation whereby, just as Shirley and her companions imitate an adult world (which also envies and tries to emulate them), black Africans, once they are "civilized," invariably copy the white world (itself envious of certain "black" attributes). The conceit is simply more bizarre in *Kid 'n Africa,* given that here we have a doubled metaphor which the filmmakers no doubt considered absurd on all levels: since the only thing more ludicrous than kids mimicking the culture of adults is blacks aping the culture of whites, the Jack Hays "burlesk" gives us black babies futilely copying the culture of white adults.

It is hard to disregard the early images of Shirley Temple in the cannibal's cauldron, insouciantly powdering her nose while she awaits her tiny Tarzan, when one considers the films she made two years later with one of the century's great black dancers and performers, Bill Robinson. Whatever one says about Shirley Temple's films with Robinson, none of them matches the vicious racism of *Kid 'n Africa.* What we might suggest about the Temple/Robinson films is simply that in many cases, their racist intent falls short of the mark, and at moments of shimmering reversal, the actors shatter through the film's intended ideology. For the most part, their setting puts us in a semantic framework within which its various racial and sexual undertones can function as covertly as possible.

The Littlest Rebel and *The Little Colonel* both appeared in the same year, 1935, and both take place in what might be called the primal scene of American cinematic racism (a terrain first plundered on a major scale in Griffith's *Birth of a Nation* [1915]), the Southern plantation around the Civil War, which is seen as a cultured idyll of contented black slaves and kindly white masters about to be shattered by the unruly intrusions of victorious Northerners. Indeed, this setting describes two of the four films in which Bill Robinson appears with Shirley Temple, as if, paradoxically, only the strictly defined conditions and prohibitions of Southern plantation life could furnish the sensibilities of the thirties with acceptable insulation for what we get on screen: the warmth, even heat, of an extremely intimate relationship between an older black man and a younger white girl, on the surface at least, a violation of strict racial and sexual decorum (it is interesting how often the arrival of an authority figure ends Temple/Robinson dance numbers: there is guilt and embarrassment on all sides, as if their "having fun" were actually a deeper kind of offense).

Their first film together, *The Little Colonel,* takes place shortly after the end of the Civil War: the titles, projected over a plantation house photo, say "KENTUCKY IN THE 70s." This is of course the historical period addressed in *Birth of a Nation,* except that here there are no carpetbaggers, mulattoes, reconstructionists: plantation life seems to have continued smoothly as before; emancipation has not altered anything for the blacks, and least of all for Bill Robinson (here named after his chief employment: "Walker"). When Shirley's mother Elizabeth (Evelyn Venable) marries a Yankee with the provocative name of Jack Sherman (John Lodge), Shirley's arrogant and irate grandfather, the Confederate Colonel Lloyd (Lionel Barrymore), disowns her. We hereby have the disruption of the family structure that is the premise for most of Shirley Temple's movies, and certainly the precondition for the paternal interventions of Bill Robinson.

As the film progresses, Shirley (often obnoxiously) persuades the Old Colonel to recognize his own character flaws, and reconcile his differences with Shirley's parents, in the process helping them to outwit some ruthless con men. The Colonel's change-of-heart is figured as a spiritual redemption catalyzed by Shirley's earlier participation—as the only white spectator—at a black riverside baptism. She later re-enacts the baptism in a mud puddle with her two black playmates, Henry Clay and Lily, using her grandfather's sheets (in a scene reminiscent of the KKK "sheet discovery" scene from *Birth of a Nation*) for their baptismal garb. In this scene, we see Shirley "blackening" herself both literally with the mud and figuratively by assuming the blacks' religious ritual (seeing his muddy granddaughter, the Colonel says she looks like "poor white trash," even though she is actually muddy—black—below the waist!). By playing "Deep River," the baptismal spiritual, over the end titles, the soundtrack underscores Shirley's role as "bridge" between worlds (William Faulkner uses a similar tactic with the white idiot Benjy's attendance of the black church service in his 1929 novel *The Sound and the Fury*), and the blacks' role as the spiritual authors of the white family's "happy ending."

The colonel's conversion comes not just inductively, after the black baptism ritual, but also directly, upon his realization that his granddaughter is just as stubborn as he is (or, to reiterate the inversion that

53

is at the center of Shirley Temple's films, that he is acting like a child). By taming her irascible grandfather in the end (the last reel, which is the only one in color, actually improves upon the idyllic state of the opening), she is only continuing what in the film is a long series of triumphs over adult ignorance and intolerance.

At the start of the film, Shirley is declared to be a "Colonel" by the head of the Union company with these words: "completely unarmed— except for your golden curls, brown eyes, and your dimples, you've captured an entire regiment . . . this one." She receives her "commission," and dismisses the soldiers. So many of her films show Shirley Temple in (quasi-)military situations, that one might wonder to what end a little girl is so often seen, albeit parodistically, in charge of regimented adults. One might perhaps look to the effect of increasing world tensions in the thirties in Europe and in Asia, but martial references in these films are always displaced: Shirley commands toy soldiers (as in the final number of *Rebecca of Sunnybrook Farm*), black children (who she calls "my men" in *The Littlest Rebel*), or Union soldiers here. Since Shirley Temple's mythic stature derives in part from the gravity, importance, or pure size of the adults whom she "plays with," "charms," or manipulates—in this film, big black women (Hattie Mc-Daniel, the maid, who lets her steal some forbidden cookies); Union soldiers; the big black man, Robinson (who holds in neutered abeyance the sexual threat represented generally by the black male); and the authoritarian Colonel himself—it is likely that the martial references and her dance routines with Bill Robinson serve similar purposes, being but special cases of her ability to get her own way with adults, to "capture" both their attention and their obedience.

If Shirley is able to plunder blacks' most useful attributes, her charm in this picture comes at the direct expense of the blacks who surround her. The most unappealing scene of the film comes on the way to the riverside baptism. Mom Beck (Hattie McDaniel) and Walker are accompanying Shirley, and, in order to disguise the hard truths of her parents' financial desperation, they play the standard adult game of spelling words out rather than saying them. Predictably, this action lays them open for revelations of black malapropism and illiteracy ("food" is spelled "f-u-d-e," "money" "m-o-n-i-e," and "poorhouse" "p-o-h-o-s," and when Walker fails to recognize the latter spelling, Mom Beck says "ain't you got no education?"). The contrast between the super-articulate Shirley, on the one hand (it is but one of the implausibilities of the film that she in fact does *not* understand what is being spelled out here!) and the blacks' seemingly intractable verbal clumsiness on the other again lays out for the spectator the film's distinction between Shirley's behavioral childishness that can be outgrown and the blacks' constitutional infantilism, which cannot.

Despite their verbal backwardness, blacks in the film are apt, if not indispensible, surrogates for Shirley's shattered family structure. We never actually see her playing with anyone other than the black kids, Henry Clay and Lily (she even manages to convince the Colonel to give what he calls the "pickaninnies" a ride, with their wagon hitched to his horse). After he almost upsets a vase in the beginning, Walker seems uneven as a servant, yet he (even more than the black maids) consistently serves as a discreet conciliator and mediator in the Colonel's feud with his daughter, and provides Shirley relief from the Colonel's aloofness and callousness, even at some risk to his own position.

It is proper to ask, however, what the relationship is between the blacks in the film themselves: where are the parents of the black children, and what is the relationship between Walker and the women on the plantation? The contacts between Mom Beck and Walker, at least are nothing if not fussy and contentious. At one point, Mom Beck offers to tell Shirley "a black story about my first husband" whom she despised. With insufficient males, caustic females, and unparented children the apparent norm for blacks, it is no wonder that we see no intact black families, and that every black adult in sight seems delighted to become a foster-parent for Shirley. Here, as elsewhere, the black self-sacrifice that keeps the white family intact seems to require the sacrifice of the black family.

The most compelling scene in the film, the amazing "staircase dance," comes just after the Colonel has brusquely told Walker to put Shirley to bed, and ends with his reappearance at the staircase, unbraiding his butler and his granddaughter with an apt "what's going on around here?" In fact, the staircase dance prefigures the pattern

of every subsequent Temple/Robinson number: Robinson demonstrates an aspect of black culture, and Shirley imitates it: "I want to
do that, too." After he has shown her "a brand new way, how to go
upstairs" and their gravity-defying *pas de deux* is over, he says "tomor-
row, I'll show you some more steps." It is the first time in the film
that Shirley, full of "charm" and "spunk," has herself been charmed
by an adult (although, as we have seen, the racist reading of this scene
would simply be that one permanent "child" is charming a temporary
one). Without warning, though with great conceptual cushioning, we
witness the (in the context potentially explosive) spectacle of male and
female, black and white, old and young dancing in exquisite concert,
a black male's way of tricking a reluctant white female into bed. Spectators could savor their deepest fantasies and their worst fears in one
and the same image. So much did they love the dual resonance of
this scene that the Temple/Robinson dance partnership was an instant
hit, and a variant of the "stairs" dance was included in every subsequent
Temple/Robinson film.

The interesting thing about this number in particular, and generally
all the Temple/Robinson tap dance numbers, is that she's not so much
dancing *with* Robinson (the *pas de deux* paradigm, played to perfection
in the dance routines of Fred Astaire and Ginger Rogers), as dancing
like him; the routines are not designed as a man/woman couple dancing
out their feelings towards one another at all, but as an exercise in
education and imitation; pedagogy, not romance, is the fruit of these
encounters. Yet these are strange lessons in which the student learns
and mimics the exercise as the teacher is demonstrating it for the very
first time! One dancer (Robinson) teaches an apprentice (Shirley) steps
which, however, she seems to already know. This impossibility derives
from a political/ideological requirement. Blacks may be in debt to
white culture for some things, but they are also subjugated by it in
every way; here, the film's message must be to show Shirley (and white
culture in general) being in the cultural debt of black culture without
actually being subjugated by it.

These numbers are really planned, then, as *synchronous*, rather than
complementary dancing. But that too makes sense in that the star, Shirley, is, as we have seen, magnified in proportion to the magnitude of

the people she gets to mirror, obey, or admire her. Although the scripts suggest that Bill has taught Shirley the steps, and that she is simply learning and repeating them, since they are dancing at the same time, it is visually ambiguous who is imitating whom; from a certain point of view, Robinson could almost be seen as a "projector" for (projection of?) Shirley's figure, darkening, enlarging, and deepening it, tying it to the tradition that he represents. Even though he has first taught her the steps, his presence is solely for her benefit, and he is solely at her disposal (see the end of *Rebecca of Sunnybrook Farm*, whose last shot is a close-up of Shirley, editing out any final glimpse of Bill Robinson, with whom she has been dancing for several minutes, and who presumably is still beside her in the last shot).

Yet despite these structural constraints, the genius of the Temple/ Robinson combination erupts in these routines, and no moviegoer could fail to see, despite the political limitations imposed upon their editing and choreography, that Shirley Temple and Bill Robinson were engaged in an artistic intercourse with a momentum and rhythm that set its own rules, and that virtually exploded the racist myths of the film narrative that surrounded it.

The Littlest Rebel, which appeared after *The Little Colonel*, towards the end of 1935, might be called the ideological prequel to *The Little Colonel*. It tells the story of Shirley Temple's Confederate father, Captain Herbert Cary (John Boles), who escapes from the Yankees aided by the Yankee, Colonel Morrison, whom Shirley has charmed, and who has a daughter "just like her." Soon, though, Cary is recaptured, imprisoned, and sentenced to death. Only through the personal intervention of Shirley and Bill Robinson with Abraham Lincoln (Bill Robinson's deference is so overdone, that he wipes his palm off on his coat before shaking hands with the Great Emancipator!), do Shirley's father and the Yankee colonel receive pardons.

The elements of these first two Temple/Robinson films, are amazingly similar. Either external (the Northern army) or internal (personal strife) disorder threatens the white family structure. In both cases, Shirley's character's mothers are sincere and loving, but impotent, while the (grand-)fathers are obsessed with principles outside the family (duty, honor), are unfeeling and insensitive, or are simply absent.

In both the black characters are as important narratively as they are undervalued societally. The plantation setting features what seem an uncountable array of black pickaninnies and retainers who far outnumber the visible whites on the plantation. Indeed, *The Littlest Rebel* opens with the standard shot of black kids chasing and falling off a carriage that passes through the plantation gates (*Birth of a Nation* was the first major American film to use this visual conceit—*Song of the South* [1946], *Show Boat* [1936], and other movies repeat it almost exactly), and from then on, there is virtually a black person in every plantation scene (albeit without narrative stature). It is peculiar that here, as in *The Little Colonel,* we never see black families or significant relationships between black men and women. Blacks are not here for themselves, clearly, but mainly for others, and more precisely, *for whites.* In this film alone, they—among other things—set up elaborate scouting networks to allow the Confederate Captain Cary to slip past Union lines, preside over the secreting of household items, and organize Mrs. Cary's funeral.

The casting, then, already sets up in visual design what we later learn from the plots: in all four films that he made with Shirley, blacks (and particularly Bill Robinson) are instrumental in helping the Shirley Temple characters overcome disruptions to their families (in *The Littlest Rebel,* once her mother has died, Robinson actually helps save her father's life), but apparently at the cost of their own ability to aid and form bonds with their own presumably non-existent family members.

Despite *Littlest Rebel*'s plantation setting, and its sizable black population, we have, in lieu of any intact black family model, a limited smattering of "darkie" types: Bill Robinson (called "Uncle Billy" here), responsible, loyal, generous; Willie Best (in *The Littlest Rebel*), shiftless, lazy, and mentally deficient; Sally Ann, Shirley's black contemporary; and so on. (Here, as in *The Little Colonel,* there is a peculiar studio racism in the discriminatory cast credits whereby the black actors are lumped together below the white actors, such that even the black star, Bill Robinson—who certainly comes just after Shirley Temple in box office appeal—does not receive second billing, but, must appear below the least significant white cast member).

The film begins with the customary establishing shots of antebellum blacks working in the fields, and the standard Negro spiritual soundtrack. But the blacks we shall get to know are the "house niggers." Uncle Billy and Jim Henry (Best) are the servants at Shirley's birthday party in the first scene, and visually tower over and overpower her, flanking her chair, but are obviously at her service (coded by their bodily stance of bent backs). After Shirley's birthday guests have their ice cream, she asks them: "how would you like to see Uncle Billy dance?," and Uncle Billy performs for the assembled kids, while Jim Henry plays harmonica. In fact, the dance is not really for the kids, which would be a relatively harmless affair, but for the adults watching the movie. This point becomes clear when Jim Henry's harmonica is soon supplanted by the full "adult" 20th Century Fox orchestra. We are the "kids," free to enjoy watching black humiliation and powerlessness (would Uncle Billy have been able to say "no, not now, I'm tired"?) without needing to ask "adult" questions about its moral implications.

In fact, Jim Henry does refuse to dance, but, again, the reasoning here is purely ideological: it's not that he has the right not to dance, but that, as he slurs: "the body's willin,' but the feet just stays too close to the ground," a mind-body split that will plague Henry later, when Uncle Billy asks him why he is trembling when the Yankees come near: "My mind say they ain't gonna hurt me, but my body don't believe it." It is, of course, useful in a system where the body is ruthlessly exploited, and the mind systematically deprived by law, to assert the myth that blacks are by nature and not by design so dissociated.

So the opening birthday party scene serves more an ideological than a narrative purpose, establishing the two contradictory, but standard, cliches about black males both before slavery: on the one hand, a willingness to perform backbreaking (as in the opening credits) or humiliating tasks at the simple behest of even the youngest white person; on the other hand, a laziness that renders them useless to anyone, least of all to other blacks. A similar device is at work in the portrayal of the white Union soldiers—Sargent Dudley is the rude, boorish, and insensitive Yankee soldier type of Griffith films, whereas

Colonel Morrison is honorable, even-handed, and upright—but to a far lesser degree than with blacks. Robinson and Best represent the dichotomized, even schizoid image of the black in the white imagination, and the salient fact seems to be that the roles are plausible neither separately nor in combination.

Right in the early birthday party scene, the film also sets up Shirley's *need to imitate*, which, as we have seen, is a key part of her filmic presence. But, as in *The Little Colonel* and the later Temple/Robinson films, this need soon translates into a *need to imitate blacks*. What larger cultural need is she carrying here? Simply white America's traditional form of what might be called "exclusionary emulation," the principle whereby the power and trappings of black culture are initiated while at the same time their black originators are segregated away and kept at a distance.

In the next scene, Sally Ann gives Shirley a handmade golliwog (self-representation?) for her birthday, but gets tongue-tied and tremulous at the idea of wishing Shirley "happy birthday" at all (Butterfly McQueen's film characters also suffer from a similar defect)—this extreme self-effacement and awe on the part of the taller, older black girl, of course, augments Shirley's mythic stature as the figure of leisure and beauty for whom blacks must work and to whom they also must defer. We then leave the blacks on the porch outside the house and join the children inside, dancing the minuet in a mock-adult ball, a scene derived directly from typical situations in the Hays "Baby Burlesks" (the transition is made by a minuet on the soundtrack that overlaps the earlier scene with the blacks). Thus, we re-enter the culture of pseudo-European Southern gentility which white children are already mastering, in direct contrast with the black children on the porch, who are forever incapable of even approaching it (at best, producing grotesque parodies of it, as in *Kid 'n Africa*). Interrupting the formal dance, and the way of life that it symbolizes, is the news of the Civil War's outbreak, which furnishes an occasion for more ideological overlay. As Uncle Billy explains the War to Shirley:

"I hear a white gentleman saying there's a man up north, who wants to free the slaves."

"What does that mean, 'free the slaves'?"

"I don't know myself."

Uncle Billy, who seems satisfied with plantation slavery, and who is skeptical about Lincoln (whom he will later meet) and his "emancipation" schemes, represents one pole of opinion. But the more accurate viewpoint is put into the mouth of the less reliable speaker, Jim Henry. At one point, Jim Henry says that only Southern whites need be afraid of the Yankees: "They won't hurt us 'cause we slaves; dey's fightin' for us, but if you'se white and Southern, den you'se the enemy." Uncle Billy, of course, reacts by saying "ah, don't pay him no mind . . . "

Aside from discrediting any black aspiration to leave the plantation, the Robinson/Best dichotomy allows the worst kinds of racial stereotypes to be vented without, however, completely undermining Robinson's heroic status. The characterization of Jim Henry is so distorted here because it cannot share its load of racial calumny with Robinson. Jim Henry (a relatively tame version of a character that Willie Best recreated through several more or less ignominious films) ranges from mental confusion to shiftlessness to irrelevance—in fact, it is no range at all. The latter attribute—the tendency of black servants to digress, which Butterfly McQueen made into her trademark—is a humorous theatrical device that goes back to Sophocles, but receives here a coding that is not individual, but racial. When showing initiative (Jim Henry thinks of bringing water for Captain Cary to wash his face), these servants usually get it wrong (Shirley reminds him that this was her idea), or find their suggestions rebuffed (he thinks of shining Cary's boots, but Cary orders him to do something else).

Even in their subservience, blacks are expected to show some initiative, but Jim Henry cannot properly manage either subservience or initiative (did it never occur to the filmmakers, or even the slave holders, that such behavior, if it ever existed, is a remarkably clever way of dealing with an impossibly oppressive state?). He digs a trap for the Yankee troops, but falls into it himself, he marches, as one of Shirley's "troops" in a mock regiment of black children (to spite the Yankees, Shirley has reversed her commands; Jim Henry stops when she says "company halt!," and she chides him, again, for getting things wrong). Finally, Uncle Billy and Best accompany Shirley in her efforts to gain justice for her father, and at one point are seen shining shoes (far from the plantation, with only one charge, blacks seem predisposed to shine whatever white person's shoes are handy—here, *both* of them are seemingly caught at the moment when they are shining Shirley's shoes: how many pairs did she take with her?). Jim Henry asks the properly Wittgensteinian question "why is a shoe called a 'shoe'?" and is again chided by Robinson for stupidity.

Uncle Billy is an even more important figure here than in the prior film (the very name tends to merge Bill Robinson's actual and cinematic identities): he is at times both a surrogate mother and a surrogate father for Shirley; he supplants and acts for each white parent at times, and at times for both of them, yet he is servile as well as parental (certainly every child's fantasy is that their parents exist only to serve their needs!)—by the end of the film he becomes her man-servant, brushing her clothes almost incessantly, and taking up the slack for the deficits in her life; he is the only other person, besides Shirley, who enjoys the privilege of a private meeting with President Lincoln. Her relationship with Uncle Billy, her act of blackening herself with shoe polish early in the film, and her hiding out with the other black kids in the secret closet establish Shirley as member of both white and black family structures. When her mother dies, she is buried in what is notably an all-black funeral (the only other white person there is Shirley's father), attended by at least forty blacks, singing, appropriately enough for Shirley, "Sometimes I Feel like a Motherless Child." Her dance routines with Uncle Billy—the longest is performed in order to raise money for the train fare to Washington (Uncle Billy's "Negro" ticket is, of course, less than Shirley's child's fare)—are more extensive here than in *The Little Colonel* (though one of them contains an unmistakable reference to that film's "staircase dance"), and a no less remarkable cementing of the kinetic bonds between the older black man and the young white girl.

Yet, though identified with blacks, Shirley retains all of the privileges of whites. We have a quite striking scene—an example of the double-valence of the film's imagery—when the blackfaced Shirley is ordered by Sargent Dudley, the "bad Yankee," to take off his boots. Instead of doing so, she commits what would otherwise be an intolerably defiant action for a black: she takes his leg and pushes him onto the floor! Only later, after chasing her ("Come here, you little black rascal"), does Dudley inadvertently wipe off the disguise, and reveal Shirley's true race.

In the end, Shirley's mythic stature has led her to conquer not only all the blacks, but also most of the Union Army, and its Commander-in-Chief, President Lincoln himself. If the film's obvious moral is that "we grownups haven't as much sense as you children," the film's more subtle product is the realization that while Shirley has gotten Lincoln to emancipate her father and Colonel Morrison, the emancipation of blacks about which Uncle Billy was so skeptical is nowhere in sight. From the evidence of subsequent years, as portrayed in *The Little Colonel,* the "happy ending" does not seem to alter anything, and proports only to restore the skewed moral underpinnings of its initial narrative context.

The last two Temple/Robinson collaborations, *Just Around the Corner* (1938) and *Rebecca of Sunnybrook Farm* (also 1938) take place in a Northern setting, and are generally more heterogeneous, and less compelling than the "Southern" films. Whereas these earlier melodramas could be safely sequestered at some mythical time in the past, the Northern films—replete with Depression concerns and themes—had to be contemporary in order to be credible (there is also a kind of discriminatory regionalism involved here, whereby the South is always seen as representing the obsolete, antiquated "past," whereas the North is pictured as the modern, enterprising present and future). Big band music supplants Southern harmonica and banjo. Great ingenuity had to be spent on figuring out how to include the by now mandatory Bill Robinson without getting into too much detail about the oppression of blacks in the North. In *Just Around the Corner,* he plays a doorman, who manages to get away for some production numbers in the basement. Yet interestingly, the pretense slips in the final dance sequence (during the kids' benefit for "Uncle Sam" Henshaw) in the "Walk in the Rain" number, where he and Shirley pick cotton, discarding the Northern persona and reverting to Southern paradigms.

In *Rebecca of Sunnybrook Farm*, he plays a farm hand—less plausible, but close enough to stereotypes of Southern blacks to work dramatically in a Northern setting.

In many ways, the repressed racial tensions of the two Southern films are translated into highly diluted airings of repressed class issues in the Northern ones. *Just Around the Corner* is the quintessential fantasy of the deposed Depression-era middle- and upper-middle class; a "riches-to-rags-to-riches" narrative. Shirley's father has literally gone down in the world. He is an erstwhile engineer now employed as a handyman in his own swank apartment building in New York, where he has been forced to move from an upper floor to the basement. Through Shirley's intervention, and through romancing the bank president's niece, he is able to complete his building and return to his former class status. *Rebecca of Sunnybrook Farm*, similarly, brings Shirley, down on her luck after the death of both parents, good fortune through the magic of radio, as she is first discovered, then lost, and then finally re-discovered as first choice for a cereal manufacturer's radio campaign featuring "Little Miss America."

Of the two, *Just Around the Corner* touches most explicitly on class antagonisms in the North. Shirley, as the daughter of the handyman, has become interested in Milton, the nephew of the banker (whom Milton refers to as Uncle Sam; Shirley's misunderstanding of this reference allows the film to make some statements about patriotic altruism through Shirley's misguided—but on the symbolic level laudatory—actions on behalf of Milton's "Uncle Sam"). When he invites her up from downstairs, she is shunned by Milton's mother and the other kids ("she even has to cook," one of them says). Another plot feature, less emphasized, is the gradual resolution of tension between white and black working class represented by Gus (Bert Lahr) the chauffeur, and Corporal Jones (Bill Robinson), the doorman. Completing this "lower-class" family unit are a chamber maid, Kitty—who is Lahr's female counterpart and serves to normalize and balance the Temple/Robinson pairing—and a group of lower-class kids, taken straight from the *Our Gang* comedies (or even the "Baby Burlesks") and reprising their standard kids' imitations of gangster movies.

The film's "class act" is the quite remarkable "benefit," which Shirley stages to raise money for "Uncle Sam" (who her father has told her needs help). The incredible structural significance of this benefit (which contains the bulk of the musical numbers in the film) is that we have the lower-class element in the film—the hotel staff and the kids—getting together to help the same "Uncle Sam" (either the "real" Sam Henshaw, the cranky capitalist, or the American economic system itself) that has betrayed them in the first place. Once more, then, the potentially liberating potential of this most powerful symbolic coalition—the working classes, the blacks, the youth, and, most of all, the omnipotent Shirley Temple herself—is diluted and deflected to support a comfortable and conservative norm. Thus, the film tries to have it both ways: Shirley's children's rebellion is also a collaboration, and the now "emancipated" blacks concerned cannot even think of bettering their position (one underlined in the extraordinary "Brass Buttons and Epaulets" number, in which the doormen from the finest hotels in New York join Bill Robinson for a tap-danced homage to the "honor" of their lowly positions) if the lower-class whites, whose advancement in any case would have to come first, seem so content in theirs. The working classes' relationship to the white upper classes, then, South and North, ends up being sweat-mediated, whether the work is picking cotton or entertaining (as we have seen, the "benefit" features numbers in which Robinson does both).

Despite all this, however, Bill Robinson's presence seems to alter and even warp the tight ideological nets cast around him. His entrance, dancing down the art deco staircase in the early number, "Anyone Can Sing this Song," is one of the most explosive moments in Shirley's films, literally shattering the tepid complacency of the duet that proceeded it between Shirley and Kitty. Perhaps most remarkable here is that Robinson feels no need to *ask* permission to syncopate the banal rhythms of the number: he virtually barges into the white grouping, dancing into the circle in such a way as to make clear that his feet and his musicianship are his admission ticket.

Similarly, some of the best Temple/Robinson dance numbers appear in *Rebecca of Sunnybrook Farm* (particularly the "Have You Heard?" number at the end, with Robinson in soldier's uniform), despite their seeming irrelevance to the plot. The theme of class conflict is subordi-

nated here to a moralistic division between city and country, represented by Shirley's sleazy step-father and his "girl" on the one hand,
and the wholesome relationships of Anthony Kent and Gwen Warren,
and Shirley's Aunt Miranda Wilkins and Homer Busby on the other.
Shirley actually begins her rise to fame and fortune in the country,
aided by technology in the form of a telephone hook-up that allows
her to broadcast over the radio from her disapproving Aunt's home.
The Northern pastoral ideal here does not diverge substantially from
the Southern one, except perhaps in that there is less justification for
Bill Robinson's (here, "Aloysius") docility and subordination—except
of course the ideological belief in the natural and eternal inferiority
and subservience of black people.

The film's final shot, in which Shirley's dance with Robinson cuts
into a frozen, knowing close-up of Shirley alone, sums up the final
place where the four Temple/Robinson films have arrived. Robinson
and Temple have reached their peak—fittingly at the top of a set of
stairs (quoting the *Little Colonel* staircase dance)—and at this point the
camera cuts out Robinson, and Shirley's image is left, distilled out of
her prolonged tutorial with the carrier of black cultural prowess,
looking greater and larger-than-life; despite all pretense at plot, the
films have all along been there to magnify a star who, although she
would only have two or three years of effectiveness left, would have
lent an indispensible aura of indomitability, rebellion, and even "soul,"
to countless subsequent white female stars three, four, and even five
times her age. Fading almost as it is shown, the image of this childhood
commander of a racially mixed squadron of soldiers has on retrospect
a melancholy prescience, as if that shy smile were both a kind of
farewell to her own career as well as to an entire decade and era of
America's moral, and even racial, innocence, an innocence that World
War II would soon forever destroy.

5

Angel, Venus, Jezebel: Race and the Female Star in Three Thirties Films

Mae West: *I'm No Angel*

It seems a great distance, in many ways, from Shirley Temple to Mae West, but finally, both are involved in the project of outwitting the male-dominated world with childish gusto. The real scandal of Mae West's characters is not their unapologetic sexuality, but that they manage to get so far using it. The final courtroom scene in *I'm No Angel* (1933), in which West becomes her own defense lawyer, underlines the characteristic impotence of male institutions in the face of West's impertinence. The disruptive power of West's sexual demeanor is a mature form of Temple's breaches of decorum, and it is interesting that West, like Temple, made an early career in burlesque of merging the worlds of adult and child, appearing in one review under the billing "The Baby Vamp."

Mae West achieves much of her sex-goddess stature with the complicity, and even encouragement, of black women. Swarthy and elemental, black women can elevate by contrast West's white and ethereal beauty. The scenes of the maids adorning West with various articles of clothing—black nymphs to West's blonde Venus, suffused with the same aura of scandal that greeted Manet's *Olympia,* in which a black servant waits on a courtesan modeled after Titian's *Venus of Urbino*—are classical instances of the "black maid(s) dressing or grooming white woman" sequences, which reach their pinnacle six years later in the

12. *I'm No Angel*. Mae West and her black maids. The dominant "I" and the coded "other."

famous dressing scene between Vivien Leigh and Hattie McDaniel in *Gone with the Wind*.

It is true that these blacks—as in the case of Shirley Temple—do not ultimately share in the benefits of the mythification that they have made possible, but West (who wrote the story and scripted much of the film) still conveys a remarkable sense of co-operation across racial lines. Insofar as all of West's films are about consolidating women's power in spite of a limited social context, it is difficult in them—unlike the Temple films—to consider any woman, black or white, as the ultimate inferior of any male, and that is what makes them finally more revolutionary.

"Beulah, peel me a grape," perhaps the most famous line in a film full of famous lines, seems to be an order directed at a generic black maid called "Beulah." It might be taken that way if uttered by a white male "master." But West's maids are not consistently obsequious, and her interactions with them are often strangely chummy. It might be said that if some white actresses derive their aura of purity and chasteness by opposition to the dark and earthy black maids who surround them, then West's image benefits by her kinship with, rather than her difference from, the same kinds of figures. As coded in these films, particularly of the thirties, the black maid and hand-servant is usually the antithesis of white female beauty, but it fits in with West's overall design to use these figures as darker counterparts, rather than as unaesthetic opposites. So when West looks over her shoulder and says, referring to Cary Grant, "My man's got rhythm," and the giggling black maids say "Yes'm, I knows what you mean," West commits a certain breech of racial taboos in order to share both the terminology and presumably the content of sexual secrets of white and black male "rhythm." It is difficult, in fact, to tell whose grape is really being peeled.

I'm No Angel reveals the conventional forms of the mistress-servant relationship in movies of the thirties by exaggerating them. In the scene where West is trying out her sumptuous trousseau, for instance, the maids attending her have a contrasting semiotic function. They wear the laced cloth tiaras that one associates with maids' dress codes, whereas West's bridal garb features a huge golden tiara, which parodies both her own narcissism and the gap created between black and white by the difference in the coded value of the tiaras. One of the main reasons for West's legal vindication is that the jury believes Beulah's favorable testimony about her mistress—how could a black maid not be telling the truth, given the prevailing sense that blacks are actually too simple-minded to be deceitful? Maids' utterances are typically suffixed with a stereotypical "Yes, ma'm" or "No, ma'm"— but as parody. The standard pose of racial obeisance seems as silly as the conventions of male dominance which West constantly punctures. The practice is made to seem so extreme that, during the trial, Beulah inadvertently says "yes ma'm" to the male defense attorney!

Marlene Dietrich: *Blonde Venus*

The mythic stakes in this 1932 movie are at least as high as in *I'm No Angel*—higher, in fact, because whereas Mae West's self-mocking attempts at mythic enlargement obviously involve hyperbole, Marlene Dietrich's Josef von Sternberg-crafted persona (Helen Faraday) is meant to portray a normal housewife and mother, propelled by purest accident into a life of extreme degradation and extreme elevation. The first images we get of Faraday involve her bathing her child, sewing, and putting the child to bed. "This could happen to any white woman who loves her child," the screenplay seems to say, whereas the visual rhetoric of the film, by contrast, makes Dietrich into a blonde goddess who supersedes and suspends all of the obstacles which hinder and frustrate the average woman or man. The title itself contains an implicit linkage between beauty ("Venus") and whiteness ("blonde"). Even though Helen Faraday's career takes her into realms of metaphorical and actual darkness, her blonde beauty encodes an internal brilliance, which eventually overcomes that darkness.

The film toys, perhaps to a fault, with a set of accustomed oppositions which Faraday reverses or merges in her own person—in chronological order: housewife/fallen nightclub star; black ape/blonde woman; chaste spouse/sex symbol-prostitute; good mother/wanted criminal; female gender/uncertain gender. Despite these various transformations, the film enlists sympathy for Faraday's quest, as it is clear that she has been unjustly persecuted, and has only committed her "crimes" in order to pay the $1500 for her husband Edward's (Herbert Marshall) European treatments for "radium inhalation."

The length and tenor of the early scenes involving the parents and their young child emphasize that what is at stake here is the preservation of the white family unit against Edward's possible death (at the very start of the film, Edward's doctor cradles a skull visibly during their conversation), and Nick Townsend's (Cary Grant) threat to the marital bond. To the extent that Helen is trying to preserve that family unit (albeit by having a relationship outside that unit, with Townsend), the spectator wants her to be the agent of the family's salvation (at whatever cost), not the object of societal persecution.

Aside from this purely narrative advantage, the figure of Helen Faraday takes on far wider connotations, aided by the film's manipulation of prevailing notions of race. Her external "blonde" beauty becomes the sign of an internal heroism, and both seem to separate the "blonde" from the "dark." Yet this heroism, as we shall see, comes from her ability to integrate into her "female blondness" the categories of blackness and maleness. She becomes an Odyssean hero whose range of experience extends to the widest possible extremes—in this case, the heroine can even unify domains of racial and sexual opposites.

The first station in Helen Faraday's (renamed "Helen Jones" by the nightclub manager) odyssey is perhaps the most shocking and the most telling, in terms of the film's overall racial and visual design. Her "Hot Voodoo" number is a rather extravagant nightclub act—though perhaps not for the thirties. The club's decor mimics the visual cues denoting "Africa" to most Americans (*Tarzan, the Ape Man,* made the same year, finally engraved these visual jungle motives into America's visual memory in a way never completely effaced). A black bandleader in a stylized treehouse conducts music heavily coded "primitive" and/ or "jungle" (drums and high syncopation). Soon a group of women in Afro wigs and dark make-up parade through the club—holding spears and shields with ostensibly "African" markings, but here, as in *King Kong,* the iconography is rather Micronesian or Amerindian than African—escorting what appears to be a large ape, which soon arrives on stage and begins to undress.

Normally, we know that the reality *beneath* an ape-suit is benign, but we never except it to be unveiled before our eyes on stage. The notion of penetrating the tabooed, primitive, animalistic bearer of blackness is titillating enough. But as the ape takes off its costume, starting at the hands, the first revelation is that quintessential object of male fetishism—the white woman's hand—emerging in glowing radiance from a hairy black ape, with the various "African" emblems undulating in the background. Next, emerging from the black, ugly, male ape's head is a white head: blonde, beautiful, and female. The scene is a classic example of mythification by comparison. It explicitly uses negative racial codings to define and raise to a higher power a white figure powerful enough to assume and yet neutralize the obscurity of blackness. Indeed, the "Hot Voodoo" scene relies on a marking of difference so extreme that the blonde Dietrich does not use her own hair, but instead wears a *blonde* Afro wig. The frizzy blonde hair,

13. *Blonde Venus.* Helen (Marlene Dietrich) in her 'Hot Voodoo' number. Mythification by comparison.

and her harmony with the "African" women in the chorus line indicate that, despite having entirely removed the gorilla suit, she has now assumed some of the attributes of her "black" get-up. Indeed, the subtle joke intended here is that, as a blonde *femme fatale,* she is conceivably more threatening to the white male than a black gorilla would be. The very ambiguity of the trope is part of its power: does every beautiful white woman have a primitive, male, black, ape-like ardor within her, waiting to be unleashed? Or is it that this particular woman is such a goddess—a "Venus"—that she both incorporates and transcends all such male-created sexual and racial fantasies? Whatever the case, it is clear that the "Africanized" blonde, figured here, soon becomes the prime symbol of the fallen Helen Faraday. Note that in the "wanted" poster that circulates after she abducts her child, she has been photographed wearing, not her own hair, but the frizzy blonde "Afro wig" from the "Hot Voodoo" number.

Even as a fugitive kidnapper, Faraday manages, whenever we see her, to have at least one black maid—in terms of the film, these maids (usually unattractive, and seemingly without children themselves) provide symbolic contrast. In Norfolk, Virginia, the maid is called "Viola", and has no real plot function, but a rather large semiotic one. Hattie McDaniel, in New Orleans, is "Cora," and she refines here her standard dual movie roles as aesthetic foil and maternal surrogate for the mythified white woman. Particularly in the latter role, the black woman acts as the supplement to white motherhood, a "stand-by" (often literally!) to complete whatever emotional or physical gaps the "blonde goddess" paradigm seems to lack. Surprisingly, the white and black women seem unified, not estranged, by their "joint custody" of the white child. As Detective Wilson (Sidney Toler) cases the area, trying to find Faraday, Cora faithfully sounds him out and reports his presence to her mistress. Throughout, the narrative cooperation between white and black women (as in *I'm No Angel*) undermines the structure of male laws and punishments, and is made to nullify any interest in the real inequalities between these women. Soon though, Helen Faraday even loses her black sidekicks, and reaches her nadir in the South, completing the symbolic journey through "blackness" and "squalor," landing without child (whom she's voluntarily returned to her husband) or money (she truculently gives away the $1500 check from her husband that was to repay his medical costs) in a shelter for the homeless.

But the very next scene snaps us abruptly to Helen's zenith: "blonde beauty" overcomes "Southern squalor." The name "Helen Jones" appears in a montage of neon marquees in different languages: the goddess's "divinity" is no longer regional (small Southern clubs) or underfunded (needing a "blonde wig"), but international, and authentic. As she appears in the Paris club dressed in tophat and tails, she exudes a suavité formerly associated only with her erstwhile suitor and benefactor Nick Townsend (he just happens to be in the audience!). What has changed is that—as the structural contrast between the earlier "Hot Voodoo" number and this one reveals—the "Blonde Venus" has now usurped, not merely black vigor, but male privilege. Here, mythification elevates Dietrich over white men as well as black women, while borrowing crucial characteristics of each. Her masculinized appearance stands out from a background consisting solely of elegantly feminine dancers. Just as savagely dressed women background dancers in "Hot Voodoo" emphasized her Venus-like purity and *whiteness,* her elegant female company in the Paris club develop that part of her image conveying strength and *maleness.* Whereas Dietrich was a warm and self-sacrificing mother previously, she is known in Paris as being made of "ice," and of doing only what is in her best interest (mentioned as if this were a major affront to men!).

Dietrich has, in fact, come full circle. In the course of becoming "well-rounded," she has assimilated and overcome the realms of white motherhood, black womanhood, black manhood (by adopting the tall, dark, primitive trappings of the gorilla), and white manhood. Truly only a goddess could exhibit such ubiquity and potency with such apparent ease. In the early scenes, she refused to smoke or drink. Now, when Townsend meets her in her dressing room, she is dressed in male clothes, smoking, and drinking. Yet to end the film with this variety of crossed codes, however, would be to unsettle entire traditions of racial and sexual etiquette.

The film, in fact, was not an immediate critical success, and that may have been because of the unbelievable ending, in which von Sternberg has Dietrich turn back the clock, and replay the failed domestic scenario. Townsend convinces Faraday to go back to her husband and child. She does so, and restores to the screen the stable images of wife, husband, and child which began the film. As she sings her son asleep, we are back in the realm of the German fairy-tale Helen tells her child in the beginning (really a disguised account of her first meeting with Edward). As she sings, and as the family triad begins to restore "normality" from the nightmare of what has been, entire visions of powerful womanhood, and of proximate and merged blackness (as well as dozens of other forms of social misbehavior) fade from the screen as if they had all along only been dreams that could air subversive social fantasies for a short time only. The blonde Venus shrinks in stature, and whatever enabling blackness and maleness she may have "absorbed" along her journey seems never to have existed in the first place.

Bette Davis: *Jezebel*

As we have already seen, the *child-like* female Hollywood star of the thirties—whether child or adult—seems to be prized in society, and crucial to many film plots. Therefore, it should come as no surprise when, in the film *Jezebel* (1938), Bette Davis (Julie) angrily asks Henry Fonda (as Preston Dillard, her fiancé) why he treats her like a child. He responds: "Because you act like one—a spoiled one . . . " Julie answers: "You used to say you liked me like that once: you never wanted me to change . . . remember?"

This strange interchange highlights the quandary of such an ideal, which wants from the idealized white woman an adult ability to preserve and obey social norms, on the one hand, and a childlike capacity for periodically ignoring or breaking those constraints on the other. In effect, Preston is criticizing Julie here for *obeying* his orders, precisely when such orders call for the disobedience of other orders— for acting like a "spoiled" child. Whereas the film *Jezebel* generally blames Julie for her own behavior and its results, her exchange with Preston points out precisely the double-bind which is certainly the more pertinent source of the film's tragic ending.

Since much of the plot of the film hinges on the question of command and obedience, it is perhaps no surprise that the "childlike" blacks play a prominent role throughout the film, conveying, among other things, an early sense of institutional servility in the culture of "New Orleans 1852." The "plot of obedience" literally enwraps the film's narrative, right up to the ending, when Julie virtually commands Amy, Preston's Northern wife (Margaret Lindsay), to stay behind while she accompanies Preston to the dreaded "Lazarette Island," the place for the hopeless "yellow jack" victims. If Miss Julie represents "childish disobedience" (punishment is threatened, but never executed by white males), then the blacks that surround her represent "childish obedience" (punishment threatened and executed), repeating the interracial dynamics of the Shirley Temple movies, but with more dire results.

The first words of the film are: "Boy: stop here . . . ," yelled by Buck Cantrell (Preston's rival for Julie's attention) to a black carriage-driver. Minutes later, another carriage-driver, pulling guests up to where Julie lives with her mother, doffs his hat, repeating "yowsm" ("yes, ma'am") to his passenger's orders, which are so frequent that he continues saying "yowsm" mechanically even after the guests have already gone inside. Although this initial servility seems merely a cause for laughter, it actually strikes the dominant thematic chord of obedience for the entire movie.

Later (still within the first five minutes of the film), Julie arrives in her riding garb, and is literally surrounded by black servants. Three of them take care of her horse, others rush in front of her to smooth the way. She arrives at her own party scandalously late, and without changing her clothes, but is still fussed over—while walking!—by at least a half dozen servants. The abundance of blacks here certainly exaggerates Julie's social *distance* from them, but also in some ways illustrates her absolute *dependence* upon them. When Julie wants to deliver an irate message to Preston (a long meeting has delayed him), she gives it to "Stymie" (the child actor also seen in the *Little Rascals* series), the "hapless black messenger boy," who obediently, if confus-edly, conveys it to Julie's fiancé. (One wonders how the South ever prospered, since in films it sends its messages by invariably incompe-tent blacks.) Other blacks help her make her toilet, in scenes taken right from the typical "grooming and dressing white women" convention. It is noteworthy that Julie's hand-servants are extremely light-skinned, as if her dominion spreads over all conceivable hybrid skin shades (much in the manner of Dietrich's racial omnipotence in *Blonde Venus*). Several black waiters serve drinks in the film (in the party scene and the scene of Dillard's board meeting, "the black waiter with the drink" becomes, for the camera and for the participants, a point of continuity and linkage). Everyone knows his place, and obeys the convention. Uncle Cato (Lou Payton), like so many of his kinsmen, seems to suffer from mind/body dissociation. When Preston says "you haven't forgot-ten how [to mix a mint julep]," he says "the head might forget, but the hand remember." When Preston asks Uncle Cato, on the "special occasion" of his return, to "join me in one," the social distance must be maintained, and Uncle Cato is well trained. The black waiter refuses, since "it ain't hardly proper" for blacks to drink with white people, but he does offer to drink it in the pantry, saying blessings for Preston and his wife.

Even if this amazingly labor-intensive and servile environment bears some resemblance to historical reality, the actual purpose is not mimetic, but rhetorical and comparative: the obedience of the black world heightens the profile of the white one by contrast. Whereas the white New Orleans world's attributes are "relevance" and "mastery" on the positive side, they also include "obstructiveness" and "vindictiveness" (as in the reliance on "dueling" to settle affronts) on the negative side. Blacks provide an excellent foil in this film, continually denoting "irrelevance" (or comic relief), "subservience," and "facilitation." The best example of the latter, is the "carriage is a-comin'" scene, when long chains of black watches joyously pass along the news of Preston's return (mirroring with great emotional exaggeration Miss Julie's hope that he will not relent and marry her). During the charged dinner sequence at Halcyon Plantation, the background space in virtually every sequence is filled with images of black servitude, as if to provide a harmless space on which to highlight the machinations and quarrels between the white males (particularly Preston and Buck Cantrell).

With respect to the main character, Bette Davis, the contrastive function of black retainers in this film differs from the types of mythification we have seen with Shirley Temple, Mae West, or Marlene Dietrich. Here, the purpose is not solely to enlarge Bette Davis's screen image (though this aim is also served). Rather, the *over*-proliferation of black assistants in *Jezebel* seems to make the narrative point that Miss Julie is in many ways *un*admirable, as if the superfluity of black hands and faces surrounding her, over which she has some control, were meant to symbolize her increasing surplus of vanity, over which she has almost no control.

The film's strong emphasis on the coding of servility by color exactly parallels the earliest conflict in the film, which is also about codes of

77

14. *Jezebel.* Julie (Bette Davis), "an abundance of blacks," and a red dress. The coding of servility by color.

coloration arbitrarily set by society: Miss Julie disobeys norms of coding virginity by wearing a red and not a white dress to the society ball. She has bought this dress to get back at Preston for putting business (male priority) ahead of her (female priority). (Interestingly, during a "dressing scene" with her black servant, Julie offers the gown to her once she has used it at the ball, although she knows that "red" denotes "prostitute," as if the whites' "white/red," "virgin/whore" distinction is not seen as concerning the black.) Julie manipulates Preston into taking her in the red dress, and ultimately manages to alienate him. Clearly, if Miss Julie (childish and disobedient) could break at will whatever codes of color displeased her, then things would be on the verge of breakdown in no time at all. As threatening as it no doubt is to substitute "red" for "white" (how does one then distinguish a "virgin" from a "prostitute"?), substituting "black" for "white"—although presumably on the minds of many of the servants who pass across the screen—is never even mentioned as a possibility (after all, how would one then distinguish a "master" from a "servant"?).

On a certain level, the film seems to be depicting the foolish consistency of the highly artificial New Orleans aristocracy, without however allowing a serious criticism of its racial politics. Indeed, rather than exploring further the nature of social sign-systems, the movie truncates its own political proof-text in favor of a quasi-theological moral. The blacks would be no longer irrelevant beneficiaries if color codes were to self-destruct here. Julie's obedience to Preston's child-like ideal for women ("you liked me like that") leads her to further acts of social disobedience (at one point after Julie learns that Preston has married a Northerner, Julie's mother must admonish her that "you can't fight marriage"), acts which, left unpunished, might threaten the entire racial and sexual edifice of obedience.

For this reason, the film's narrative ties up the two loose ends in one plot movement. Julie's disobedience receives punishment, even as blacks are removed from any possibility of being re-coded as "command" instead of "obedience." Julie gets what is coming to her, but is not totally unredeemed—unlike the Biblical "Jezebel," her prototype: "the corpse of Jezebel shall be as dung upon the face of the field . . ." (2 Kings 10:37). Instead, the blacks revert to their stereotypical film roles as spiritual midwives for the ethical "rebirth" of previously disruptive characters.

At the point of highest tension in the film—when Julie has provoked Buck Cantrell into a duel with his former apprentice Ted, and she realizes that the mischief she has precipitated is now out of her control—we get her rebirth: the "Halcyon Plantation" blacks (who also typify Hollywood's "halcyon" view of antebellum plantation life) assemble on the porch in a "spontaneous" spiritual outburst. Miss Julie (akin to Shirley Temple in her unquestioned control of plantation blacks), sits down, gestures, gathers them around her, and leads them in an incongruously joyous spiritual. The blacks are rendered once more "irrelevant" and "oblivious," serving the sole purpose of casting (in this case religious) significance onto the "white plot." Finally, Julie regains some control, but only of an illusory sort: she can conduct the black chorus, but cannot alter the conduct of the white males she has incited to action. She has even worn the "proper" white dress to impress the (unknown to her) already married Preston, but too late.

Her "baptism by fire" at Halcyon ("That's why I wore my white dress tonight . . . I'm bein' baptized," she says) is achieved against the background of black, anonymous, ecstatics, and in her first "mature" action, she sacrifices herself to certain death at the side of Preston, the man who had first asked her to never stop "acting like a child."

Miss Julie in the rest of the film is a completely changed person: she leaves the refuge of Halcyon's white world and merges with the tumult of disease and sickness in New Orleans—signified by various images of blacks, especially the visual predominance of bare-chested blacks in the ambulance brigades. She nurses Preston alongside a black woman, and finally has "the chance to prove I can be brave and strong and unselfish." She in effect becomes more black the less selfish she becomes, though many would prefer the more brash Julie, given that she—and many other Southern women of her type—was all along just obeying orders. She leaves New Orleans for "Lazarette Island," no longer distanced by social class from the black servants who surround her. Now, as Preston's servant, she is paradoxically at her most independent. She has been equalized with the black sanitary workers, the leveling effects of disease making a mockery of all arbitrary color codes.

6

Trimming Uncle Remus's Tales:
Narrative Revisions in Walt Disney's
Song of the South

Song of the South (1946) represented for Walt Disney and his still evolving filmic enterprise a considerable technical and financial advance. It was his first major box-office hit after World War II, and indeed was one of the most successful films of 1946. *Song of the South* continued the stream of popular children's features by Disney Studios that had begun in 1937 with *Snow White and the Seven Dwarfs* and had included a series of critically acclaimed movies such as *Pinocchio* (1940), *Fantasia* (1940), *Dumbo* (1941), and *Bambi* (1942). Even more ambitious than Disney's prior films, *Song of the South* featured some of the most stunning cartoon animation and color techniques yet seen. Yet it did not restrict its efforts to animation; it also carried to maturity Disney's earlier experiments in combining live actors and cartoon characters on screen. The cartoon segments, approximately one-third of the film's total length, illustrate three of Joel Chandler Harris's *Uncle Remus* tales, and bring to fulfillment a long-held private desire of Disney's, as he stated in an interview of 1946: "Ever since I have had anything to do with the making of motion pictures, I have wanted to bring the Uncle Remus tales to the screen. They have been in my mind from early childhood."[1] The remaining two-thirds of the film consists of the "framing" story, the relationship between the black servant, Uncle Remus, and Johnny, the grandson of the plantation

81

15. *Song of the South.* Uncle Remus (James
Baskett) and Johnny (Bobby Driscoll).

mistress. By these ratios, it should already be clear that the film brings
much more than just the *tales* to the screen.

Plot Summary

The story is compelling, poignant, and, as Disney reformulates it,
closer to the facts of Harris's life than to the Uncle Remus stories.
When the film opens, Johnny (Bobby Driscoll) has been brought to
live with his mother (Ruth Warwick) and grandmother (Lucile Watson)
at the latter's Georgia plantation. He does not realize at first that his
parents are separating, and he is greatly disturbed when his father
(Erik Rolf) says "goodbye" to him. Later that evening, he decides to
run away to Atlanta, where his father is a newspaper editor (these

events roughly parallel the early life of Harris). As Johnny sneaks away, he hears Uncle Remus (James Baskett), a kind old black man, telling the story of Brer Rabbit and the Briar Patch. Remus offers to run away with him, but stops first at his cabin for food, and diverts Johnny with his fables. As he begins, the cabin seems to dissolve into a brilliant blue sky, with Uncle Remus walking with animated cartoon figures, singing "Zip-a-dee Doo-Dah." Soon he encounters Brer Rabbit, and the all-cartoon narrative of the first fable begins. Its moral is that "you can't run away from trouble—there ain't no place that far." The boy decides to return home, and his mother blames Uncle Remus for his interference in the matter.

Johnny begins to make friends, with Uncle Remus as protector and support. He meets Toby (Glenn Leedy), a little black boy on the plantation, and Ginny Favors (Luana Patten), a poor white girl who lives nearby. Ginny is quite well behaved, but her brothers are rowdies who bully their sister and everyone around them. When they threaten to drown a brown puppy she has found, Ginny gives it to Johnny, and a fight ensues between him and the brothers. Uncle Remus protects him as well as he can, and later tells him the story of Brer Rabbit and the Tar Baby. Again, Brer Rabbit uses psychological trickery to outwit his foes. Later, Johnny uses the lessons he has learned from the tale to trick the brothers. Out of revenge, they tell Johnny's mother that he has been consorting with Uncle Remus again, and again Uncle Remus is scolded.

Johnny's mother wants to lift his spirits with a birthday party. He invites Ginny, but when he goes to pick her up, he has another confrontation with her brothers. Ginny, also brawling, ends up in a mud puddle. Neither Johnny nor Ginny wants to go to the party now. Uncle Remus comes upon the two dejected children and cheers them with another Brer Rabbit story. The three return to the plantation and Johnny's mother blames Uncle Remus again for making the children late for the party. She forbids him from speaking to Uncle Remus again.

Uncle Remus, heartbroken because his good intentions have been misunderstood, decides to go away. Johnny sees him riding away and rushes to catch him, crossing through a pasture where he is attacked and seriously injured by a charging bull. Johnny's illness causes his

16. *Song of the South.* The rhetoric of harmlessness.

mother to send for his father. They reconcile their differences, but Johnny remains in his delirium despite his father's presence. The parents convince Uncle Remus to come and see the boy, and he is able to comfort the boy with another story. Soon, Johnny recovers, recognizing his father, now reunited with his mother. The film ends with a now-recovered Johnny romping along with Ginny and Toby, singing "Zip-a-dee-Doo-Dah," and able to conjure up the cartoon characters that until then only Uncle Remus had been able to animate. Uncle Remus runs to meet them, and they all dance blithely into the sunset.

Children, Blacks, and "Harmlessness"

More than perhaps any other genre, animated cartoons encourage the rhetoric of *harmlessness*. The "winsomeness," "adorability," "charm," and "cuteness" of Disney's cartoons refers in the first place to their content (there is, of course, the "Road Runner" mode, in which cartoons become a veritable workshop of cruelty) but secondly to the way in which the cartoon is to be taken. For even if the cartoon is violent, cruel, or deceitful (as the Disney cartoons typically were not) it is not expected to have any serious extra-cinematic reference or effect. In other words, the cartoon is *ipso facto* innocuous, even if it really is not; we tend to condescend to cartoons, just as many adults condescend to children. From this standpoint, what could be further removed from serious racial and sexual issues than the children's feature? Cartoons, like the children who watch them, are out for unpretentious, light entertainment. Often cartoons are even "shorts," as if lacking the weight and breadth to take up more than a fable's time span. Adults might chaperone children to see such a movie as *Song of the South,* but cartoons, it is thought, are mainly for relatively unsocialized "code-naive" minds. Even cartoons with overt political content would seem on the surface to escape the problem of realist films, which usually invite comparison with reality through their photographic *verisimilitude.* In cartoons, there is a clear separation between the fictive and the real; indeed, our contact with animated film seems to entail the premise that we do not take it too seriously. One would think therefore, that, even more than the horror or monster movie, cartoons would have a right to be taken as *pure entertainment,* beyond all psychoanalytic or ideological access. Yet—as Aesop's and The Grimm brothers' tales are not the only texts to remind us—this seeming harmlessness is far from the actual state of things.

Despite the enormous popular appeal and reach of Walt Disney's films, the above considerations prevented, at least in the early days of his career, serious scrutiny from being brought to bear on the ideology of his cinematic products. A film such as *Song of the South* invites at least some political comment, if only because of its major emphasis on "live" action, and its placement amidst one of the more thorny political issues of American history, one whose effects and implications (which the film unsuccessfully endeavors to conceal) have even today not yet reached their full course.

Aside from the traditional European iconographies of "black-evil/

85

white-good," which Disney had already used in all his work (particularly in the film *Fantasia*), Disney had employed explicit racial codes only once before, in a sequence from *Dumbo* in which some crows sing their astonishment at seeing that Dumbo, an elephant, has flown up into a tree. One film critic remarks of this scene that the crows "are undeniably black, but they are black *characters*, not black *stereotypes*."[2] Whatever the case, Disney seems to have had no second thoughts about transferring some of the Uncle Remus stories to the film format. Disney's own words indicate that he did not understand or acknowledge the racial ambivalences underlying Harris's tales as a major issue—and in this respect, he was hardly unique. The figure of Uncle Remus—like the similar figures "Uncle Tom" or "Uncle Ben"—have had a long and until recently untroubled history in the white American psyche. Uncle Remus, the literary creation, came into white children's lives with the same guarantee of harmlessness as his filmed portrayal.

Yet *Song of the South*, far from being an innocuous childhood drama, gives us one of the best imaginable elaborations of some deeply revealing and disturbing American fantasies about slavery and blackness. Through the prerogatives of its designation as *pure entertainment*, it has been generally able to deny the seriousness of its subject's (Uncle Remus) position and tribulations. The film covers over the slavery problematic with an unbroken insistence on satisfying young and mature viewer's appetites for a flattering fantasy. As Leonard Maltin suggests, political objections to *Song of the South* "are ultimately defeated by the film's sheer entertainment value."[3] Yet the very attempt to camouflage the political is itself political, and soon becomes an aesthetic quandary, distorting the overall semiotic vocabulary of the film.

Omission: The Fading of the Black Narrator

The aesthetic faults with Disney's "plantation film" issue directly from its historical distortions. Indeed, almost every review of *Song of the South* (even by the most sympathetic critics) mentioned one factor above all as problematic in what was otherwise a technical *tour de force*. *Variety*, for instance, noted that the film was "sometimes sentimental, slow and overlong . . . the real story [using live actors] . . . overbalances the three cartoon sequences, and could be cut . . . " Bosley Crowther of the *New York Times,* pretending to chastise Disney face to face, complained that there was too much "live action": " . . . although we have anxiously tolerated your previous 'live action' escapades, we have never particularly admired them . . . Almost two-thirds of the picture is mundanely performed by actors as in any Hollywood movie . . . "[4] There was critical agreement that most of the children in the audience (as well as the adults) found the framing story, the parts that involved live action, extremely slow, in contrast to the extremely interesting cartoon sequences. Yet if we look at the Harris tales, we will find that the space allotted to the actual Uncle Remus stories vastly exceeds the narrator's descriptions of the story's setting. In the original tales, the *content* of the tales, then, is far more important than the *context* in which they are told; Harris (who once referred to himself as a "dull reporter" of the tales he had picked up as a child from a black plantation bard) calls as little attention as possible to himself as secondary narrator, "the little boy" who listens to Uncle Remus. The energy of Harris's narrative divides between the connivances of Brer Rabbit and Brer Fox and the cunning crafts of Uncle Remus's own dazzling storyteller's acumen. As one writer says, " . . . dwarfing any . . . nostalgia for the old agrarian South, any apology for slavery is the enormous shadow of Uncle Remus cast upon the cabin wall. *The setting was created for him, not he for the setting* . . . the center of the stage is always his."[5]

Yet, bringing Harris's tales to the screen, Walt Disney made a radical artistic decision: to invert the relationship between the space allotted to Uncle Remus's stories and the narrative that presents them. At the same time, as we have seen, he decided to increase radically (and unhappily) the ratio of "live action" to "cartoon" sequences, an extreme move that met with almost universal disapproval. One may perhaps clarify what seems to be a harmful and arbitrary alteration by supplying the political undergirding for these oppositions: 1) "cartoon/live action"; 2) "Uncle Remus's tales/Johnny's plantation experiences." The third and decisive opposition remains unspoken: 3) "black narrative voice/white narrative voice." The balance clearly tilts in favor of the black discourse in the original tales, but reverses in the Disney film.

To be sure, there are scenes where the opposition breaks down—where "live" actors interact with the "cartoon" characters (as in the transition to the "Zip-a-dee Doo-Dah" song), but these transitions, too, are both visually and funded by the trappings of the "real" or "white" narrative voice (literally, in the case of the various "numbers" that blacks are made to sing). The film, in effect, bends over backwards to put the act of black narration/oration "into its place"—or, at least, to put it into a place conventional and acceptable to white viewers. The result of expanding the context and shrinking the text of the Uncle Remus tales is, quite simply, to remove the black narrator Uncle Remus and his Afro-American narratives from "the center of the stage," making him and his tales merely an adjunct for a story of a different sort. Symptomatically, even in his title, "Song of the South," Disney leaves completely undecided the balance that will be struck between the folkloric material ("song") and the film's setting or context ("south").

While in their original form, the Uncle Remus tales already contained contradictions, in the big screen version these contradictions were amplified. Both Harris and Disney held a fantasy view of plantation life, one which Bosley Crowther in his *Times* review accurately described as: "a sublimely unreconstructed fancy of the Old South . . . with the Negroes bowing and scraping and singing spirituals in the night . . . one might almost imagine that . . . Abe Lincoln made a mistake." (Needless to say, the happy compliance of the servant in his or her socio-economic degradation and exploitation is a fantasy of the master, dominant class, perhaps, but has never been the reality of slavery.) Even were this picture a reliable version of antebellum conditions, it is an anachronism in the narrative of the Uncle Remus tales, as Harris and Disney portray them, for they are supposed to be set in the *post-bellum* period! Harris, in his introduction, asks us to "imagine that the myth-stories of Uncle Remus are told night after night to a little boy by an old negro who appears to be venerable enough to have lived during the period which he describes—who has nothing but pleasant memories of the discipline of slavery . . . "[6] In other words, the reader/viewer is asked to believe two fictions at once: that pre-war life on the old plantation was a time of happy conviviality between black and white; and that the upheavals of the Civil War have done nothing to change this state of affairs—the former fiction is balm for the credulous, the latter a refuge for the desperate, possibly even for those Southerners and Northerners hoping to efface by nostalgic denial a reality that could not be faced. Whatever the case, the need to conceal the actual dangers and pressures facing Uncle Remus flattened his portrait into the form that Disney has taken great pains to "fix" in film forever.

It might be argued that the removal of the narrator is a formal peculiarity of film in any case. As in much modern fiction, the film's narrator seems to have vanished, and the story seems to tell itself. Even more so than implied by Jean-Louis Baudry and others, it seems clear that our sense of film narrative "refers jointly to the action of an implied narrator . . . and to the imaginative action occasioned by his placing and being placed by the spectator."[7] We accept that the film is "narrating" to us the same story that Uncle Remus first narrated to the boy. The boy, then, would transfer his function as "reporter" to the film, which erases both his and Uncle Remus's voices (although this is literally not the case, since Baskett's voice is used for Brer Fox and, in the last sequence, for Brer Rabbit). Yet this loss of the present narrator intrinsic to film does not account for the imbalance in the space allotted to the stories themselves.

Marking: Coding the Plantation Black

Harris's main interest was the story content, combined with the tension and brilliance of Uncle Remus's art of narration (or what Gérard Genette would call *récit*). Disney's film replaces a black narrator's insights about freedom, endurance, and cunning with a certain approach towards *mise-en-scène*, a highly coded Hollywood setting, derived from a string of "Old South plantation" movies reaching back through *Gone with the Wind* and *Jezebel*. For most of the film, then, the audience must wade through the visual luxuriance of an extravagant political mythology—its excess seeming, in fact, a failed compensation for its questionable substance. The removal of Remus from the *storytelling authority* tends to imbue him rather with a certain *iconic utility*. As we

89

have seen previously, "marking" blacks takes the form of seeing them not as individuals but as a group with a certain "character" or "nature." Remus becomes, not active storyteller, but passive symbol of the semic codes that the whites around him would have him bear: "comforter," "mediator," "wise and benevolent," "faithful," "long-suffering," "cheerful," "harmless." In the final attribute, we can see that the implicit connotation of the film itself has begun to infect its major characters. The film becomes less descriptive than prescriptive, enclosing in one person "the race of which Uncle Remus is the type" (Harris's description)—a truly harmful message wearing the garb of harmlessness.

The particular visual design of both the live and cartoon sequences does not at all derive from the editions of *Uncle Remus* with which Disney was familiar (a press photo shows him reading the 1921 edition with the two child stars). All American editions after 1892 featured the illustrations of Arthur Burdette Frost, which, like their text, portrayed mainly scenes involving animals. Of the narrating environment, there are, at most, occasional scenes of Uncle Remus and the boy inside the cabin. There is little of the lavish idyll that permeates the film. The film's true narrator is, in fact, the paraphernalia of "Old South" coding that we already have seen. Once more, cinematic pleasure comes, not in recognizing the veracity or verifiability of movie events, but in applauding their very *recognizability*.

Almost immediately in the film, we encounter signifiers of mythological happiness between blacks and whites. The opening titles, set against rustic engravings of the Old South, already provide a guiding discourse for what we are about to see: "Out of the humble cabin, out of the singing heart of the Old South have come the tales of Uncle Remus, rich in simple truths, forever fresh and new." Notice here that the entire issue of race—while touched on obliquely in the adjectives "humble" and "simple"—remains unspoken. The "singing heart of the Old South" is here race-neutral, precisely the opposite of how the "Old South" typically categorized its reality, from the trivial to the significant. Are these singers white or black? And does it make a difference? As we already know, all dwellings in the South are not "humble cabins"—what accounts for the differences in the way people

90

live? Moreover, there is an attempt to account for the a-historicity of the story by implying that the filmic story, like Uncle Remus's stories, are "timeless" ("forever fresh and new").

No sooner do the titles disappear than "Aunt Tempy" (Hattie Mc-Daniel) appears, riding in the carriage with the white family (now enroute to the grandmother's mansion), seemingly enjoying a comfortable and proximate relationship with them. This scene alludes to an early scene in *Show Boat* (1936)—indeed, the same actress plays the maid. Aunt Tempy is a creation of Disney's film and fulfills a purely conventional requirement. The figure of Uncle Remus alone would not have been enough to signify "Southern plantation," because the filmic code requires the appearance of at least one, and preferably more than one, maid (interestingly, the male servant is not enough: even as early as *Birth of a Nation,* at least one woman had to be represented among the black workforce, as if to cancel out tricky questions of sexual need and opportunity). The blacks on the carriage are seemingly contented, "sympathetic," or "warm and gentle"; the ones we see in the distance are busy bearing loads of cotton (there is cotton everywhere!) on their backs, driving mules and wagons, hoeing earth, and are similarly satisfied with their employment.[8] Next, the camera reveals hosts of black children (in plantation films, black children always vastly outnumber white ones—certainly this impression is both a comment on the myths about black fertility, but it also says something about the labor needs of the plantation economy: it is unlikely that all these children, excluded from schools and learning, spent the days frolicking, as depicted). As the wagon pulls up to the plantation, black children scamper up to it, grab on, and then fall off (the "pickaninnies falling" motif is copied exactly from a scene in front of Stoneman's mansion towards the beginning of *Birth of a Nation*).

Other immediately recognizable codes are aural: we have the by now familiar "campfire meetings," as in the 1929 *Hallelujah!*, with blacks—identifiable only as an indiscrete mass—singing spirituals (actually the dubbed voices of white singers, singing songs not from the "heart of the Old South" but from the pens of Hollywood songwriters). There is also the question of *dialect.* The dialect that Disney's blacks speak does not remotely resemble the (relatively more accurate) notations reported by Harris. Instead, we hear a standard cinema black dialect, one denoting simply that *this is a Negro speaking*. Interestingly, the accurate representation of the blacks' dialect, crucial to Harris's project, gets completely flattened by the film's insistence on a "singing heart of the Old South"—by not mentioning race, the film refuses to account either for the origins of the tales (Africa) or for the reasons why they are narrated in the way that they are.

The most interesting codes here are facial. The black face is marked here, first to be as black as possible, but also to be both endearing and somewhat grotesque. In this film we have a curious intensification of the usual signifiers of black facial gestures: the graphic design puts great emphasis on dark interiors and exteriors, and so "flashing teeth" and "bulging eyes" have a more acute visual aspect than is typically the case. When we first go from "live" to "cartoon" narration, Uncle Remus's face leans in and seems to fill the screen in a terrifying surfeit of blackness. Certain children were frightened by this scene, and, as *Grimms' Fairy Tales* best illustrates, the figures—pixies, fairies, gnomes, wizards—bringing benefits to the young questor are regarded as both beneficial and unearthly. Many fairy-tales feature a kind of reversal in which the good helper-figure initially seems menacing or even hostile (as in the 1939 film of *The Wizard of Oz*). By being potentially threatening, their threat canceled for the moment, the appeal of these figures for the youthful hero (and reader) is enhanced, and their guardianship seems all the more miraculous and precious. The *Variety* reviewer noticed the curious effects of Uncle Remus's face, but misconstrued its source: "James Baskett's Uncle Remus, with his fat, round black face . . . is also as warming a portrait as has been seen in a long time." But as well as "warming," the face—also echoed in the extreme rotundity of Hattie McDaniel's face—fills the screen, and seems to stand for the containment of the overall peril and mystery of a blackness which neither the children nor their parents will ever fully measure.

It is exactly in the removal of threat from the personality of Uncle Remus (in making him *harmless*) that the insidiousness of his portrait lies. He is kind, even maternal, to the son of the person who dominates and oppresses his life, a son who will, barring a social cataclysm, certainly continue this "special relationship" with his own sons. In the original stories we see him "taking Miss Sally's little boy on his knee, and stroking the child's hair thoughtfully and caressingly."[9] One can perhaps imagine why the members of the master's family might hold to a beneficent and generous set of values, Uncle Remus's stance, in light of his enforced poverty, seems imbecilic, cowardly, or falsely pacifistic. Yet it is also true that James Baskett's rich portrayal gives us an extremely *positive image*. One contemporary black reviewer noted the "truly sympathetic handling of the entire production from a racial standpoint."[10]

Yet concentrating on "the image" alone overlooks both the *dynamism* and *contextuality* of racial coding. We must regard *Song of the South* as a classic case (a precursor of *Lilies of the Field* [1963] in this respect) of the dangers resulting from a blind insistence on "positive images" for blacks: "the exact nature of 'positive,' first of all, is somewhat relative: black incarnations of patience and gradualism, for example, have always been more pleasing to whites than to blacks."[11] The "positive" features of the Uncle Remus character failed to impress many blacks and whites in 1946. The image of the benign old slave darky—certainly abnormal after the Civil War, and probably also before it—was nothing short of insulting in 1946, a time when blacks returning from service in World War II were just beginning to consolidate their hard-fought gains and agitate for their rightful place in American society. At the film's New York premiere in Times Square, dozens of black and white pickets chanted "We fought for Uncle Sam, not Uncle Tom," while the NAACP called for a total boycott of the film, and the National Negro Congress called on black people to "run the picture out of the area."[12]

Lingering Doubts: Racial Ambivalence, Class Conflict, Family Strains

The problem in the "Uncle Remus" myth is not Uncle Remus's "*character*" or "*essence*" but his *reactions*, taken as a paradigm for how people such as himself—he is the "type" of his race, as Harris reminds us—should react to their circumstances. The "plantation model" for racial relations had, and to some extent continues to have, a strong effect on day-to-day racial assumptions and behavior. The visualization of that plantation in a mass medium such as film has had devastating effects upon the nature of mass beliefs and assumptions. Disney's blacks depend almost exclusively on the whites around them, and show no signs of political awareness or volatility. Their physical suppression beneath the dictates of the script may in some part account for the overall tedium of the "acted" portions of the story.

Interestingly, despite the cosmetics of the filmic narrative, Uncle Remus still cannot but be perceived as threatening or subversive by Johnny's guardians. This fact derives from the political subtext that the film has tried to silence. Because he *is* black, and blacks are rarely coded as pure negativity, but more frequently in an *ambivalent* way. Baskett plays the character with just enough mystery and even mischief that he might be, if not harmful to children, then at least a less-than-wholesome lure, teaching the heir to white values and cultures other values and other philosophies. For the white Westerner, ties to Africa and "Africanness" (such as Uncle Remus and his tales represent) seem fated to evoke the simultaneous emotions of desire, fear, attraction, and abhorrence.

The flattening effects of the a-historical and a-political narration—aside from reducing the importance of Uncle Remus as a narrator, and the stature of individual blacks as characters—also make the ending of the movie somewhat incomprehensible, both for the children who might not be expected to pick up its sly intimations, and for the adults, who might. The three elements of social tension and contradiction that the plot refuses to address, or addresses by ignoring, are 1) social class; 2) race; 3) the breakdown of the family.

The relationship between Johnny and the poor white girl who lives near the plantation (named "Ginny," as if the phonemic similarity in the children's names could somehow close their social distance) is a potentially interesting plot element. For the first time, it seems that the film is on the verge of making a social statement, both acknowledging differences, heterogeneities, and conflicts within the rustic fabric of the "South," and also asserting that people are people, no matter what their class or race, and love conquers, if not racial barriers, then possibly class ones. At times, there are brief glimpses of underlying racial tensions. We experience the stringency of class prejudice as Johnny's mother and grandmother both dissuade him from going around with Ginny (although they never verbalize the class prejudice at the root of their admonitions). We also note the hesitation in Uncle Remus's resolve to defend Johnny from Ginny's "poor white" brothers when they want to drown a brown puppy (the color code "brown" here represents a pervasive threat in the film represented by the poor whites, a threat to do violence to the "brown" Uncle Remus and to blacks in general). There are, in effect, two taboos broken in the confrontation with the brothers: the taboo against Johnny's and Ginny's relationship across class barriers; and Uncle Remus's brashness with the white boys who are nominally his social superiors. His offense is made somewhat less acute by the fact that the boys are young and poor, but it points to an underlying conceptual problem in the Southern system: the relative ranking of poor whites (slaves to the ruling class in all but name) and blacks (coded inferior by skin color, but often beneficiaries of the privileges of proximity to the master and his mansion). Indeed, the conflict lightly touched on here between poor white and poor black fills up much Southern literature and history. But *Song of the South* makes it, typically, into a matter of personalities and prerogatives—finally, we side with Uncle Remus because he is both a "better" than Ginny's brothers, and their "elder."

The ending of the film simply omits any signs that this crucial class conflict remains unresolved. The utopian future (accompanied by the strains of "Zip-a-dee Doo-Dah") features Johnny, Ginny, and Toby (the black boy) romping up the crest of a hill, soon to be joined by Uncle Remus. This happy union of aristocratic white male, poor white female, and poor black male points ahead to some future reconciliation of classes and races. The aristocracy and the proletariat will marry away their differences, and the black will continue to trail along behind them. Unfortunately, this felicitous union leaves out two very important parties: aristocratic white woman (the "Southern belle"-type, represented by Johnny's mother and grandmother) and the black woman. Toby will be mateless, as will Johnny's prospective upper-class girlfriend. We have simply reconstituted in this conclusion the conditions for the white male's sexual paranoia (with regard to the "mateless" black male) and the Southern belle's sexual frustration (she remains in the house, while her husband finds his pleasure elsewhere), the standard opening of numerous tragic narratives (and real incidents) taking place in the South.

As we have seen, *Song of the South* either completely represses or naturalizes racial conflict and inequity. Despite some plot and character development among the white characters, it is striking that in this film the characters and roles of blacks *remain changeless*. Moreover, the illusion of sympathetic concord is deceptive. Proximity does not mean equality. The children seem to interact freely: Toby and Johnny play together, have pillow fights, and share the most intimate parts of their lives, but (as one scene makes abundantly clear) Toby still must *serve* his childhood companion, pouring morning water for him, and generally rehearsing the role that will consume his adult life. The future of the blacks on the plantation seems highly questionable. Not merely the disruption of their economic and intellectual growth is at issue here. The plot in addition makes clear that even a distantly possible redistribution of wealth (coming, in a future marriage of Johnny and Ginny, through marriage) would necessarily exclude the blacks.

The most incisive statement the film makes about Johnny's relationship to Uncle Remus, however, recalls the very process (reminiscent of slavery itself) whereby Harris first and Disney secondly appropriate and then market Uncle Remus's African narratives, without the black bard reaping any benefit from his labors. If Johnny's "black" parent teaches him the content and technique of his storytelling genius, his "white" precursors (Harris and Disney) seem in the end to have taught him the art of usurping and exploiting those stories, for by the ending of the movie Uncle Remus has been made obsolete! We (and Uncle Remus) notice with incredulity that Johnny can now bring the cartoon animals to life *independently*. As he romps up the hill, we see that he has learned to "tell Uncle Remus Stories"—an art defined in the film as the ability to conjure up cartoons—without blacks. Uncle Remus has, in effect, made himself redundant. One must reflect on the white

American commercialization of Afro-American blues, rock, and jazz to appreciate fully this allegory of cultural plunder.

Disney's tale begins with an image of family collapse: the Southern father is leaving the mother, jeopardizing the family unit and the integrity of the male line. By the end, through the unfortunate illness of Johnny, we see the parents reconciled, and the white nuclear family revived. Yet on closer examination, there is a much more profound statement hidden in these plot events, among them, that the film actually seems to delineate the central role of apparently marginal blacks in the white family unit, and their crucial assistance in its success. In almost every tableau where significant family events are shown, the black appears as a pivot of visual and emotional support. Uncle Remus, more than even Aunt Tempy, is coded as the person who resolves crises in the white social or family structure, usually by telling a story: he prevents Johnny from running away (story of the "Fox's Trap"); helps him deal with Ginny's unruly brothers (story of "Tar Baby"); and lightens Johnny's and Ginny's despair after she has muddied her dress (story of the "Laughing Place"). Every instance of assistance meets with criticism from Johnny's elders, as if they realized the instability of their family structure, and resented Uncle Remus's (and the blacks') indispensability to that structure.

Uncle Remus's presence, indeed, saves Johnny's life, and guarantees the next generation of the planter class. In a sense, the entire plot might be regarded as a cautionary tale about what might happen if the white male (here, Johnny's father) skirts his responsibilities to wife and family. Deserting his position as father means that he runs the risk of being replaced by a black surrogate. Interestingly, it is not the presence of Johnny's father that allows him to get better. When his mother says "Son, Daddy's here," Johnny merely looks up, without recognizing his white father, and then looks away, saying "Uncle Remus, come back." Only at this stage do the mother and grandmother have Uncle Remus sent in. From the viewpoint of patriarchal prerogatives, we have here a very dangerous situation: the father-son tie is not only broken, but broken by the black (sexual) interloper. For if a white boy can be the "son" of a black man, then the bed—as well as

97

the role—of the white father has been threatened. The possibility of founding pure-white lineages based on the power of capital and its dominance over other human beings would be lost. So it is no surprise that, the black surrogate father having replaced the white father, the son improves when he takes Uncle Remus's hand (both a spiritual and a quasi-sexual influence). The sight-lines in the scene vividly depict the sense of a black presence interfering with the white father-son connection. It is no surprise, then, that in this scene, as before, Uncle Remus is not thanked for his intervention, but merely relegated to a marginal position: the boy, now conscious, hugs his father, says "Daddy," and, together with the other whites in the room, completely ignores Uncle Remus's presence.

Song of the South reveals by the coding of the black within the frame what the story that progresses from frame to frame would deny. Blacks compensate for the absence of love in the white family, but we are asked to accept that they might be more interested in nurturing the whites' families than their own. Indeed, if we look at the direction of the maid's glances when there is a choice between looking at black children or attending to the white children, the white children always receive the attention and concern. Toby is typically marginalized or left out of sight-lines when he is together with significant blacks. For example, in the ensemble shots with black and white adults, as in the front porch scene with Aunt Tempy, Toby (out of character for this film) even appears somewhat annoyed at his systematic exclusion.

In effect, the sad secret of the film is not even that the black, though denigrated, has saved the white family unit from itself, but that the salvation of the white family (threatened either by internal or external forces) has come at the cost of the black family unit. Even as blacks find a certain stature in their centrality to white family cohesiveness, one also notes a visual and actual dismemberment in the black family. The word "dismemberment" intentionally refers here to at least three different effects of the pre-Civil War and post-Civil War system of Southern slavery and segregation: 1) the emasculation which was the figurative and often literal design of white Southern males upon their black counterparts; 2) the cruel process whereby the black family unit was torn away from African cultural practices and mediations; 3) the

17. *Song of the South.* White sightlines, black exclusion.

physical separation of children from parents, and parents from each other that followed from the definition of blacks as the "property" and "chattel" of the plantation owner. These forms of dismemberment were the price the black family paid for the white family's economic, material, and even emotional, survival. It is true, then, that the freedom of Uncle Remus would have meant the death of the white heir, but it is also true that the free agency of the white heir will mean the sudden obsolescence of Uncle Remus and the gradual deterioration of his family.

7

Playing the Changes: St. Clair Bourne's
In Motion: Amiri Baraka

At forty years old, then, I was acknowledging another tremendous
change in my life. In my life of changes. (And how can you play the
tune, if you don't know the changes?)
—Amiri Baraka, from *The Autobiography of Leroi Jones*[1]

St. Clair Bourne's engrossing documentary, *In Motion: Amiri Baraka*
(1981), sets itself the difficult challenge of fixing a subject "in motion,"
freezing it just long enough in the camera lens so we can see and
understand it—yet Amiri Baraka is not just any subject, and his is not
just any motion. Baraka is Baraka, and thus the film must in fact
have two subjects: the amazingly mercurial writer called Imamu Amiri
Baraka (who "changes" names in 1967 from "Leroi Jones"); and the
background subject of the times and personalities which over the last
thirty years have shaped Baraka's life and work. Connecting these two
massive subjects in a one-hour film is the aim, and the challenge, of
In Motion: Amiri Baraka.

Baraka: The Man
Few artists, black or white, alive today, have engaged their times and
their art as aggressively as Baraka. In the course of his various

"changes," he has witnessed, participated in, and influenced the major figures and movements of American poetry, drama, and politics in the sixties, seventies, and eighties. But more than that, his life story serves as a kind of paradigm for the kinds of changes that many blacks—especially middle-class blacks—underwent during these years.

Growing up in an ethically mixed section of Newark in the thirties and forties, and transferred to a predominantly white school, Leroi Jones (as he was then called) describes himself as feeling

> totally alone and isolated . . . I was contemptuous, frightened, and awed by the tons of white students I had to see every day . . . I was now all but invisible, and when not that, the butt of something unpleasant. (p. 38)

Jones's early sensitivity to the racist structures of life in Newark and America provided the foundation for his later poetry and politics, but in the meantime, he was exposed to class and color inequality through stormy tenures at Howard University and the U.S. Air Force (being expelled from the latter as an "undesirable" for, among other things, possessing copies of the *Partisan Review*).

After leaving what he now calls the "Error Farce," Jones quickly immersed himself in the mainly white bohemian scene of Greenwich Village in the late fifties and early sixties and was quickly recognized as one of America's freshest new poetic voices. Establishing a "literary salon" (as Alan Ginsberg calls it in the film), Jones—perhaps uniquely—had access to racially and artistically diverse figures such as the writers Langston Hughes, Alan Ginsberg, Jack Kerouac, Frank O'Hara, and A.B. Spellman; painters such as Bob Thompson; and musicians such as Archie Shepp and Marion Brown. By the age of 24, Jones's iconoclastic technique and subject matter had already put him at the vanguard of young American poets. Yet his lasting contribution to the extension and expansion of black literature and culture was just beginning. Parallel developments in black music (the innovations of Cecil Taylor, John Coltrane, and Ornette Coleman) and black politics (the Civil Rights Movement and the rise of the Black Muslims) cross-fertilized with the increasingly pointed tones of Jones's poetry, creating an atmosphere of vigorous opposition to the white racism of the sixties. Not only did blues and jazz devices become more prominent in Jones's poetry, but Jones also produced some of the best analyses of black music ever written, including the extraordinary *Blues People* (1963).

At the age of 30, Jones reached the highpoint of his Greenwich Village phase. It was 1964, that incredible year for black theater which saw the premieres of James Baldwin's *Blues for Mister Charlie* and Lorraine Hansberry's *The Sign in Sidney Brustein's Window.* Jones's own output was prodigious, including a book of poems, *The Dead Lecturer,* and three plays, *The Baptism, Dutchman* (later made into a movie), and *The Slave.* By most people's standards, Jones had "made it." Despite (or perhaps because of) his "reputation of being a snarling, white-hating madman," the white literary establishment opened its doors:

> There was all kinds of interest and requests and offers and proposi-tions. It was as if the door to the American Dream had just swung open, and despite accounts that I was wild and crazy, I could look directly inside and—there—money bags stacked up as high as the eye could fly! (p. 188)

At this point, though—at exactly the point where co-optation threat-ened—Jones made a radical "change," confirming the appraisal of his lawyer in St. Clair Bourne's film; "he did not become like the majority of intellectuals in this country . . . he did not surrender to the establish-ment . . . [but maintained] his basic stand against the established or-der." If there is anything, then, that has not changed in the midst of Baraka's "motion," it is this "basic stand against the established order."

Baraka's next move was uptown to Harlem to found the Black Arts Repertory Theater/School. Despite initial successes, the Black Arts movement was sabotaged by personal and ideological strife, as well as various kinds of racist opposition. By 1967 Jones had decided to return to Newark, where he met his second wife, Sylvia, and began to practice a more directly political activism. Increasingly interested in black cultural nationalism, particularly of Ron Karenga's variety, "Leroi and Sylvia Jones" became "Amiri and Amina Baraka." During the seventies, Baraka helped topple the corrupt machine of mayor Hugh Addonizio, replacing him with Kenneth Gibson—a move that Baraka soon would regret. Despite bogus weapons charges, police beatings, FBI harassments, and doctrinal differences within his Congress of Afrikan Peoples, Baraka remained an engaged and committed presence on both the Newark and the international scenes. In 1974, Amiri and Amina Baraka moved from a stance of "cultural nationalism" to the use of "Marxist class analysis" and gave "public notice to the world of our socialism" (p. 312). Baraka's still vibrant poems now cling to a more consistent socialist ideology than before: Baraka, "in motion," seems now mainly concerned to reveal (as in the title of his 1977 play) "The Motion of History."

In Motion: Amiri Baraka

At the outset of his film, St. Clair Bourne makes clear that he is trying to capture Baraka during a tiny two-week cross-section taken out of this amazing 40-year history: "The following documentary covers the final two weeks before [Baraka's] sentencing on charges of 'resisting arrest.'" Yet he also intersperses the story about two weeks in 1981 with news footage, photographs, and interviews covering three decades of Baraka's various "changes." St. Clair Bourne uses interviews and archival materials again and more extensively in his later documentary *Langston Hughes: The Dream Keeper* (1986). The Baraka film, is both a wide-ranging overview of Baraka's past, and a minute examination of a critical moment in his recent career.

In Motion: Amiri Baraka has a virtuoso opening, surrounding us with the central signs and values of Baraka's life in compressed form, anticipating the main themes of the film through a seemingly casual glimpse of Baraka working at home. First, there is the sound of someone practicing jazz drums in the basement of a modest house. Next, we see that the youthful drummer seems to resemble Baraka, and is in fact his son, Obalaji, practicing Max Roach drum patterns. But the allusion here is also to the past: the revolution in black arts in the fifties and sixties to which Roach, as well as Baraka, were major contributors. Finally, if we look carefully over Obalaji's shoulder, in the upper portion of the frame (astute camera positioning here), one can make out a poster of none other than Lenin. In this way, the viewer can connect in a single sequence Baraka's younger days in the fifties and sixties with his ideological and familial situation in the eighties.

The "family" theme continues as the soundtrack cleverly mixes Obalaji Baraka's drumming downstairs with the sound of his father Amiri Baraka typing upstairs, establishing in the staccato clickings both the unity of generational purpose, and the connection, always present in Baraka, between music and writing. Seeing the writer surrounded by his wife and daughter in his study while he is working, at once reverses the romantic European and American paradigm of the "isolated artist" who must remain undisturbed in a lonely study, shutting out family and friends as he works, angered at the slightest interruption (as in the first scene of Goethe's *Faust*, for example). For Baraka, inspiration is immediate, communal, and non-exclusive. While he is writing, his wife presses him to buy a puppy dog for their daughter.

Unknown to us, the filmmaker is showing us the family tiff for another reason: it establishes early on how Baraka family disagreements may arise, and allows us to imagine how a similar spat may have initiated the bizarre chain of events that resulted finally in the "resisting arrest" charge against Baraka. As Baraka exclaims in the film: "you can't get sentenced to 90 days in jail for arguing in your own car . . . with your wife about the price of your child's shoes—I mean, it hasn't come to that yet!" Yet, on the pretext of "protecting" Amini Baraka from her husband, a New York City policeman actually did reach inside his car and grab Amiri, resulting—once his identity was known—in the incredible charge and the inflated sentence which we see Baraka fighting throughout the film.

St. Clair Bourne's film has an interesting visual design, but often its soundtrack is more innovative, with several overlap and echo effects that, literally, add resonance to the story the pictures are telling. The film's structure is also unusual, being divided into six segments, all of them titled after a quote from Baraka's works. We follow Baraka "in motion" throughout these segments: driving a car; reading poems; giving a speech at a "Baraka Defense Rally"; announcing a future

105

poetry reading on his WBAI radio program; picketing the offices of South African Airways; discussing a new play after a preview; finally standing in front of a court building after another stay of his sentence. At the film's end, we read the news, conveyed in small print, that "on December 17, 1981, Amiri Baraka was convicted of 'resisting arrest' and consequently served a 90-day sentence." The soundtrack conveys Baraka's final words: "We will put them on trial one day and we will see what the people's justice is . . ."

The film, then, tells two stories: 1) the retrospective story of a generation told in often nostalgic tones by famous and not-so-famous witnesses such as Ginsberg, Spellman, Joel Oppenheimer, Baraka's friends, and even his parents; 2) the story of Baraka now, an activist getting older but not softer, refusing to "surrender to the establishment," either by selling out (in the manner of Jerry Rubin) or by some spurious conversion (in the manner of Bobby Seale or Eldridge Cleaver): Baraka, still the activist writer, perhaps even (in the title of one of his jazz-poems) "The Last Revolutionary." It is a paradox of this film that, while I find the second story more compelling than the first, it is, in fact, historical biography that the documentary form does best (as Bourne demonstrates in *Langston Hughes: The Dream Keeper*). An interesting film might have been done on Baraka's pre-1981 life, or *lives*, alone, but then, of course, it would have been Baraka "frozen," not Baraka "In Motion." So one of the pleasures, and often frustrations, of watching this film is tracing the ways in which the volatile content of the 1981 Baraka story struggles against the more placid narrative of events and people now committed to history, without the two tendencies of the film ever arriving at a satisfactory reconciliation. But at the same time, it is perhaps a minor miracle that so much of Baraka's 50 years could be squeezed into this powerful sixty-minute film. And certainly Bourne and his collaborators are trying, through the film's unresolved stylistic tensions, to remind us that it is the very struggle and contradiction between past and present, form and content, tradition and revolution that motivate change. It is surely this consistent energy of unresolution that lies at the heart and soul of Baraka's greatest work.

8

Images of Blacks in Black Independent Films: A Brief Survey

Black Independent Filmmakers:
The First Generation

Even in the infancy of motion pictures, it was obvious that film, as a new way of perceiving reality, opened up entirely new perceptual possibilities, giving the eye an augmented sense of visual mastery over its surroundings, preserving events in motion for a seemingly unlimited number of future replays, performing a wide variety of functions: educational; propagandistic; recreational; aesthetic. Some idealists—Sergei Eisenstein and Charlie Chaplin among them—even thought that film would ultimately bring about a radical improvement in human understanding and communication.

It is one of the bitter ironies of American history, then, that motion picture technology, with its singular potential for good or evil, grew to perfection during the same time period (1890–1915) that saw the systematic, determined, and almost hysterical persecution and defamation of blacks and other minority groups. Early American films depended unthinkingly on theatrical precursors, propagating racial caricatures borrowed from the popular vaudeville and minstrel shows. Black skin (often represented by blackfaced whites) came to be linked with servile behavior and marginal status. The repeatability of movies—otherwise a virtue of the medium—offprinted false racial models from celluloid onto mass consciousness again and again; real viewers came to expect unreal blacks both on the screen and in the real world. Film became a hindrance rather than an aid to racial understanding, and in many cases (most notoriously, as we have seen, in *Birth of a Nation*), served as a tool of the prevailing segregationist and white supremacist dogma.

Given this background, it does not seem unreasonable to connect the birth of black independent cinema with two portentous events in the year 1896 that made black independent films not only possible, but inevitable. On April 23 of that year in New York, Thomas Edison demonstrated a major leap in film technology. No longer satisfied with his primitive "Kinetoscope" (which could only accommodate one viewer at a time), Edison introduced large screen projection, an innovation that would allow movies for the first time to reach a mass audience.[1] And on May 18, less than one month later, the U.S. Supreme Court gave Constitutional assent to segregation in the *Plessy vs. Ferguson* decision, which endorsed "separate but equal" facilities for blacks and whites, a decision not to be reversed until *Brown vs. Board of Education* in 1954. Edison's promotion of movies to a communal (and no longer private) experience, the Supreme Court's division of this potential communality into black and white segments, and the growing resentment by blacks at their remorselessly negative images in mainstream features: all these factors inevitably encouraged and necessitated the first generation of black independent filmmakers.

The term "independent film" must, of course, be used with a great deal of circumspection, especially if, as is often the case, it is polemically contrasted with "Hollywood" (therefore "dependent"?) productions. If "dependence" has traditionally meant access to Hollywood's substantial financial resources, its skilled technicians and advanced film technologies, and its ready-made distribution and marketing networks, then for many black and white filmmakers, "dependence" has been something to be desired rather than scorned. In addition, even the so-called "independent" sector customarily (particularly in recent years) depends upon the keenly sought support of private investors, foundations, and public grants. One can declare one's independence, but in film—a particularly collective and capital-intensive art form—true independence is hardly attainable, even in the most modest productions.

Yet for many independent filmmakers, the word "independent" does not refer to any such one-dimensional version of economic self-reliance. Rather, the relative financial constraints under which independent filmmakers—and particularly black filmmakers—have operated for decades have often led to a certain aesthetic and creative privilege. Vincent Canby's comment in the *New York Times* on Warrington Hudlin's *Black at Yale* represents a not uncommon misunderstanding about the nature of independent film: "*Black at Yale* is a film limited only by the resources of money and time available to the director."[2] Yet it is by no means clear that more "money and time" would have made *Black at Yale* a proportionately better film. Indeed what Canby refers to as "limitations" (which Hudlin's film shares with practically the entire line of black independent films since William Foster's *The Pullman Porter* in 1910) precisely delineate the strength of the independent film. Without the incessant and confining restraints of box-office considerations, studio agenda, and censoring boards, the range of artistic choice in independent films is potentially *widened,* rather than *restricted.*

Because of, rather than *in spite of,* limited budget and screening opportunities, the adept filmmaker can exploit his or her marginal position to present the kinds of statements and images which can go against prevailing rules and codes. Such a filmmaker can choose to refute, to parody, or merely to copy Hollywood models—as in the cases of *A Black Sherlock Holmes* (ca. 1918), produced by the (mainly white) Ebony Film Company, or *By Right of Birth* (1921), produced by George P. and Noble Johnson's Lincoln Motion Picture Company. Yet even such derivative films by black independent companies were not just slavish sepia replicas of white Hollywood; they often involved subtle, even inadvertent, critiques of white America's racial politics. Real-world *disparities* between white archetype and black copy intrude, often explicitly, to uncover unspoken political realities. Indeed, for many such films, their very technical and financial inferiority to Hollywood productions exposes the very real-life disparities between the races generally that the film's "apolitical" plot is trying to conceal.

The "independence" of the black filmmakers in the twenties was not a deliberate choice but was enforced—in every sense—by the highest legal tribunal of the land. In the first four decades of American film history, black independent films were a product of a separationist environment, which also accounted for their major market opportunity—pleasing a growing but cinematically under-represented black audience.

The first generation of black independent filmmakers was active, albeit with uneven success, from about 1910 until the late 1930s. William Foster's Photoplay Company had produced black independent films as early as 1910, but most critics agree that the first major black independent effort was *Birth of a Race* in 1918. Artistically one of the least successful, but one of the most powerful in terms of its political aspirations, *Birth of a Race* arose primarily in opposition to the radically ungenerous and laughably inaccurate depiction of black people in D.W. Griffith's *Birth of a Nation* (1915). To counter Griffith's propaganda, Emmett J. Scott (former secretary to Booker T. Washington) formed the Birth of a Race Company. After three years spent securing patchy and often unreliable funding both from black and white sponsors, Scott managed to turn out *Birth of a Race*. Scott's film matched Griffith's epic in its pretensions, exceeded it in its length, but was woefully inferior to it in almost every other respect. The intended narrative—a comprehensive history of the Negro's past, present, and future, from Africa to America and beyond—was never finished, and the film (as mandated by some of its backers) ended up seeming like a pacifist commentary on the causes of World War I. Unfortunately, this most ambitious but technically and conceptually flawed project only seemed to show that "propagandistic rebuttals to propaganda were not yet feasible, especially from an Afro-American producer."[3]

Black Independent Filmmakers: 1920–1950

But there were other black artists at work as well. Perhaps because of its idiosyncratic aspirations, the failure of *Birth of a Race* did little to halt the courting of the black audience by other black filmmakers (often financed by white co-producers) and indeed may have spurred on their pursuit of that audience. The twenties helped establish black independent films as viable alternatives to the Hollywood product. Alongside the Ebony Motion Picture Company, that produced films for black audiences but allowed little creative or conceptual input by blacks, there were comparable companies with a high degree of black involvement. The Johnsons' Lincoln Motion Picture Company was such a company which, unlike the older Foster Photoplay Company, achieved a relatively high degree of success in the late teens and into the twenties with its productions *The Trooper of Troop K* (1917), *The Realization of a Negro's Ambition* (1917), and *By Right of Birth* (1921). But the fluid imprecision of the concept "independent" becomes clear when one notes that ultimately both William Foster and Noble Johnson left their own independent production companies for the lure of Hollywood, a kind of career "crossover" that is still common among today's independents.

The Lincoln Company's productions, both under the Johnsons and their successor, Clarence Brooks, tended to emphasize black pride and consciousness, and were often explicitly political, but they were exceptions to the rule. Generally, "black" independent film companies (many of them, such as the Reol Motion Picture Corporation, or the Colored Players Film Corporation, actually organized and financed by whites) gave black audiences an image of a black middle class full of cultured, affluent, and well-mannered families more or less free from racial misery—indeed, an image conforming to the way Hollywood films typically portrayed "normal" whites as living.

The Colored Players Film Corporation is an exemplary case of a black-white joint venture which managed a high level of production integrity in its many films, including *A Prince of his Race* (1926), the temperance piece *Ten Nights in a Barroom* (1926), and perhaps most notably, *Scar of Shame* (1928). *Scar of Shame* certainly ranks among the most technically adept and thematically compelling films of the early black independent period. The film convincingly mixes black urban reference-points (slang, ghetto scenes, dress conventions) with a somewhat melodramatic Hollywood-style "social climbing" plot in which Alvin Hilliard, a middle-class composer, falls in love with Louise, a

111

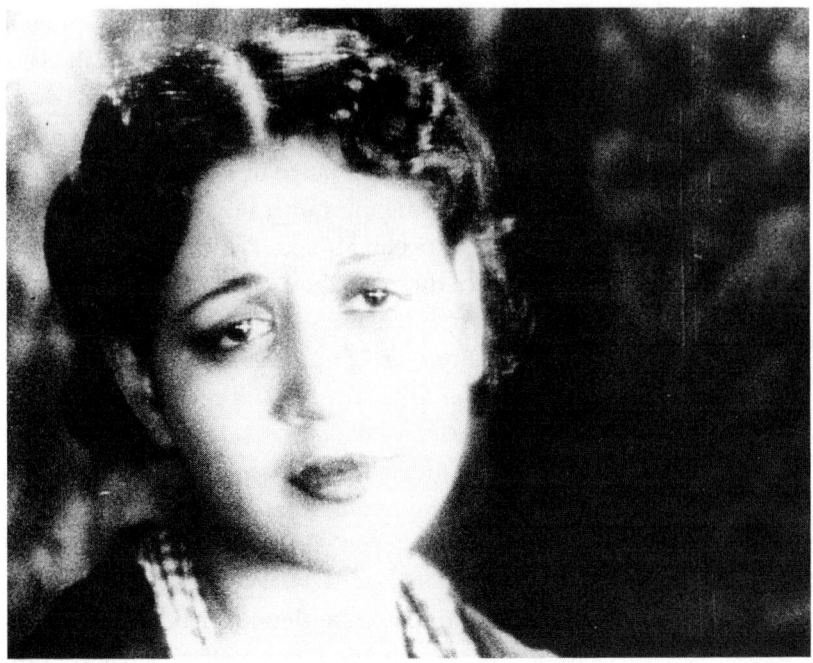

18. *Scar of Shame.* A 1928 drama of race.

beautiful lower-class girl. Their rise and eventual demise, far from having anything to do with what Thomas Cripps calls "color-caste snobbery" (if this assertion were true, then one would expect Hilliard's mother to *embrace*, rather than reject, the lighter-toned Louise; in this case, class overrides skin color), is a fairly straightforward parable of class conflict within the black community.[4] The film's iconography (for example, the "book and lamp" motto on the title cards) is often unintentionally ironic, and its symbolism all too frequently leaden, but overall, the film commands and articulates a cinematic vocabulary that sets it apart from any but the most accomplished Hollywood productions of the twenties.

Oscar Micheaux was the dominant personality of this period, and typified better than anyone of his generation the all-around "black independent filmmaker," writing, financing, producing, directing, and distributing his own films. Starting with his first feature *Homesteader* (1919)—based on his autobiographical novel of the same title—

he made thirty-three films in thirty-three years. His most provocative films include *Body and Soul* (1924)—which was Paul Robeson's first film—, *The Wages of Sin* (1929—now lost), and *God's Stepchildren* (1937). Even more than other art forms, the prosperity and even survival of a film will require it to maintain a certain pre-existing status quo. The diversity of Micheaux's films makes generalization about them difficult, but one can safely assert that, as with the Johnson brothers, Micheaux did not shy away from politically disturbing topics, even topics that might have offended some black audiences. Yet even in his less controversial films, Micheaux encountered problems that had little to do with politics or ideology. The always insufficient financial backing for his projects led to a sloppy, "single-take" aesthetic, compounded by the often insufficient attention to heavy-handed scripts, badly directed actors, and primitive handling of lighting and camera movement. These deficiencies plagued "race films" generally, and gave Hollywood films a competitive advantage, even among black audiences. By the end of the twenties, Hollywood had already begun to incorporate elements of black culture into highly polished productions such as *Hallelujah!* (1929) and *Hearts in Dixie* (1929), further siphoning off black filmmakers' potential audience. Hence a paradox arose: studio-processed and ill-informed images of blackness seemed more believable than black-sourced but technically amateurish images produced for black audiences by Micheaux and others.

Even apart from purely technical issues, the disappearance of the first generation of black independent filmmakers was hastened both by the Great Depression (which dried up sources of financial support) and by the advent of sound films (which sent the costs of production far beyond what most independents could afford). Most of their films have disappeared as well. The record of these films has been irretrievably damaged: all prints deteriorate with time, and few black independent producers could afford to make replacement copies, so time's effects have censored what even a racist environment could not, and of the hundreds of early black filmprints, only a small fraction survive today.

Despite the large numbers of all-black "race films" produced in the thirties and forties, there were only a few remarkable examples of

113

independent black filmmaking in the period. For the most part, with the new resources of sound film, black productions relied on routine musicals or melodramas with little political or social substance. Among the foremost black directors of the thirties was George Randol, who produced and directed (with Ralph Cooper) an independent all-black gangster film called *Dark Manhattan* (1937). The picture became a box-office hit "even though it was difficult to convince the [white] exhibitors that colored people would pay high prices to see their own race on the screen."[5] Million Dollar Pictures, with whom Randol was loosely associated, went on to produce a stream of quality films— mainly offprints of stock studio themes of romance, society, comedy, and crime. Randol's films, such as *Gangsters on the Loose* (1938), *Reform School* (1939), and *While Thousands Cheer* (1940), tended, like their Hollywood counterparts, to skirt controversial issues.

Another prominent black independent filmmaker of this era was Spencer Williams who often simultaneously served as star, producer, and director. His Amegro Films produced *The Blood of Jesus* (1941) and *Go Down Death* (1944), both examples of allegorical dramas firmly based in rural black religious and poetic traditions. Yet overall, aside from these and a handful of other films (including those of Oscar Micheaux, who had survived the Depression and moved with seeming aplomb into the sound era), the horizontal and vertical monopolization of the film industry by the major studios, combined with the introduction of noted black actors (such as Mantan Moreland, Ethel Waters, and Bill Robinson) into white films, had by the late forties all but extinguished the early vitality of black independent film.

Black Independent Filmmakers: 1950–1986

In this, most recent, phase of black independent filmmaking, technological innovations once more have conspired with political developments, but this time with happier results than in the late 1890s. The 1954 desegregation decision that overturned *Plessy vs. Ferguson* began a series of events leading from the Montgomery bus boycotts and the Little Rock crisis through the flourishing of the nationwide Civil Rights Movement and the initiation, in the mid-sixties, of the Black Power

114

movement. Black people attained a greater political and symbolic significance in the American mind than ever before, such that within only a few years their prior images in mainstream Hollywood films were rendered inadequate. Even the pioneering Hollywood "race films" of the late forties (*Home of the Brave, Pinky,* and *Lost Boundaries* in 1949) and fifties (a series of films, mainly starring Sidney Poitier, beginning with *No Way Out* in 1950 and continuing through *The Defiant Ones* in 1958) had begun, in light of the realities of the sixties, to seem sententious at best and condescending at worst. Hollywood was still unable to discern or depict the full spectrum of black American life and culture.

At the same time, technological improvements led to reductions in the price (and just as importantly, the weight) of 16mm camera and synch-sound equipment, which, together with improvements in the quality of film stock, made the 16mm format accessible to filmmakers with low budgets while making their "look" and "sound" acceptable to a broader public. The "New Wave" and *cinéma verité* movements gave a certain high-cultural sanction to the use of "real-life" subjects as raw material for independent film, and in many cases blurred the distinction between "documentary" and "fictional" films altogether, creating both an appetite and a system of distribution ("art houses," public television, museums) for filmmaking that did not conform to the visual and narrative principles of Hollywood's "classical realist" tradition.

As a direct result of the Civil Rights Movement, black students began entering university film programs and film schools in large numbers in the sixties, and—in contrast to many earlier black independents—became the politically engaged beneficiaries of a stylistic and technical revolution in the world of film. Skeptical about the ability of the mainstream American film industry to put its house in order, this new generation of black independent filmmakers decided to exploit film's full aesthetic and political potential. They set about *recoding* black skin on screen and in the public realm by revising the contexts and concepts with which it had long been associated. Many of these filmmakers belonged to the black middle class and were formally trained at leading universities and film schools. But, unlike many of their precursors in the twenties and thirties, they insisted on engaging problems that addressed the diverse experience of all segments of the black community.

William Greaves was one of the pioneers of this new movement. Starting out as an actor (he appeared in *Lost Boundaries*), Greaves soon moved into film documentary work with the National Film Board of Canada, and later with the United Nations before becoming Executive Producer of WNET's "Black Journal," a television series that turned out many of the most aggressive and engaged social documentaries of the sixties. Two of his best films, *Still a Brother: Inside the Negro Middle Class* (1968) and *Ali, the Fighter* (1971) indicate Greaves's range, technical acumen, and emotional affinity with the black community. He remains an "independent," even though he has directed and produced Hollywood features as well. Documentary and *cinéma verité* formats also attracted Shirley Clarke—best known for *The Connection* (1961), *The Cool World* (1963), and *Portrait of Jason* (1967)—and St. Clair Bourne (also an alumnus of "Black Journal"), whose television documentary *Let the Church Say Amen* (1973) set new standards for films of its kind.

In the seventies, the range and variety of black independent film-making expanded, and with it, the extent to which these films prolifer-ated newer, authentic codings for images of black skin. There were more fictional and narrative films, and, in gaining worldwide recogni-tion at Third World and European film festivals, black independent filmmakers now asserted their identity as a distinct and original group primed to contribute significantly to the history of filmmaking. A few independent films, such as Roy Campanella's *Pass Fail* (1978) even thematized the figure of the black independent filmmaker trying to reconcile an artistic mission (which involves breaking away from ste-reotyped roles) with white institutional demands to compromise or commercialize their recoding efforts. Or, in another example, the opening scenes of Haile Gerima's *Bush Mama* (1977) show black inde-pendent filmmakers in conflict with institutional authority. In this case—which was *not* staged—the L.A. Police stop and frisk a group of filmmakers merely *because* they are black men with camera equipment, graphically illustrating the threat felt by the status quo when blacks take control of their own images.

The majority of recent black independent films since the sixties have the feeling of intimate conversations between filmmaker and audience, and deal with issues *within* the black community, without special regard for a theoretical white viewer. Henry Miller's *Death of a Dunbar Girl* (1974) and *Color* (1982) by Warrington Hudlin and Denise Oliver both deal with class and color-caste discrimination more honestly, concisely, and credibly than *Scar of Shame* had in the twenties; *Suzanne, Suzanne* by James Hatch and Camille Billops emotionally mines, using Bergmanesque techniques, the story of an abused wife and her heroin-addicted daughter trying to compose a post-mortem on their recently dead husband, father, and tormentor—these are themes which the early black independent filmmakers would have treated indirectly, if at all. The viewer achieves, in the best of these films, an understanding of a complex black world from within, rather than caricature of it from without.

An important grouping of this new generation was active in Los Angeles between around 1972 and 1982. Most of these filmmakers were trained at the UCLA film school, but their films protest against the form and content of the tradition they were being taught. Their chief ambition was to rewrite the standard cinematic language of cuts, fades, frame composition, and camera movement in order to represent their own "non-standard" vision of black people and culture. Haile Gerima's *Child of Resistance* (1972) and *Bush Mama*, Larry Clark's *Passing Through* (1977), Ben Caldwell's *I and I: An African Allegory* (1977), and Charles Burnett's *Killer of Sheep* (1977) rank among the virtuoso articulations of this new stylistic sensibility. Julie Dash's *Illusions* (1982), and Alile Sharon Larkin's *A Different Image* (1982) extend the early methods and insights of the mainly male "L.A. School," integrating their unconventional stylistics and thematics with a frankly and refreshingly feminist reading of sexual and racial oppression. In their rejection of that kind of glossy technical sophistication that historically defines Hollywood's "classic realist" cinema, and in their refusal to remain on the easy surface of human relationships, L.A.'s black inde-

117

pendent filmmakers continue in the eighties to define the possibilities and limits of this second flowering of black independent film.

Black Independent Filmmakers: Beyond the Eighties

Under the rubric of *entertainment*—and with the help of unprecedented investment in pyrotechnics, special visual effects, and computerized graphics and animation—the Hollywood film industry in the eighties seems determined to suppress sensitivity and three-dimensionality under a veneer of technical gloss. The future of black independent filmmaking will more and more rely on how these filmmakers handle the competitive challenge from an increasingly monopolistic and compelling industry. The mesmerizing visual enchantments of a *Beverly Hills Cop* series or a *Star Wars* trilogy have led to enormous box-office success—most notably among black audiences. Yet even box-office breakthroughs by Richard Pryor, Eddie Murphy, or Whoopi Goldberg cannot disguise the fact that blacks are still being portrayed in aberrant and even bizarre roles that are mere descendants of paradigms set by Eddie Anderson, Stepin Fetchit, or Ethel Waters.

Towards the end of the eighties, a younger set of black filmmakers has achieved an unprecedented prominence, but it remains to be seen whether they will retain their prior artistic independence. The point can be illustrated by looking at three of the best recent black independents. Spike Lee's fine series of early films (produced at the NYU Film School), *The Answer* (1980), *Sarah* (1981), *Joe's Barber Shop* (1984), and *She's Gotta Have It* (1986) reveal a quirky, yet appealing filmic sensibility and the diverse social and economic condition of black Americans that few filmmakers, white or black, achieve. Mary Neema Barnette's *Sky Captain* (1984) and Reginald Hudlin's *House Party!* (1984) and *Reggie's World of Soul* (1985) share with Lee's films a fluent command of black and white cultural languages, and an insistence on counterposing them in an aesthetic dialectic. Instead of seeing blacks purely in terms of white norms and practices, these films show blacks securely positioned in their own environments, discussing and dealing with their own problems, ignoring or at best belittling the toys and

118

19. *She's Gotta Have It.* Tracy Camilla Johns and Spike Lee.

games of the dominant white culture. Yet these directors, among the best of the late eighties, have received substantial attention from Hollywood, and at least two of them are actively engaged in feature film production. It will be interesting to see in the coming years whether the oppositional aesthetics and thematics of their earlier "independent" films can be adapted for mass-market consumption. Some would doubt whether white Americans can ever learn to see blacks and themselves from a black, and not a white, vantage point. Lee's comedy *She's Gotta Have It* became, despite less than ideal production values, a major box-office hit across the nation, attracting a considerable white audience. But whether a mass public could assimilate the messages and the methods of as somber a film as *Killer of Sheep* is another question. And one further question remains: should it? Perhaps the greatest challenge for future black filmmakers, independent or not, is to find a way to prevent an imagistic co-optation in which an insincere, ritualized tolerance of recoded images may itself become just another way of keeping blacks out of the picture.

9

"Black Independent Film":
Britain and America

From the other side of the Atlantic, it often seems that—especially with regard to funding, distribution, and critical reception—British black filmmakers graze in greener pastures than their American counterparts. Americans had their most recent chance to see the latest crop of Afro-British films through the programs on "Black Independent Cinema: Britain and America" at University of California at Los Angeles (UCLA) in Spring, 1987, and later at "Blacklight: Chicago's Festival of Black International Cinema" in Summer, 1987. Horace Ové, Jim Pines, Maureen Blackwood, and others appeared in person to explain their films. These film presentations highlighted differences of theme between Britain and America to be sure, but perhaps more clearly, differences in terms of financing, production, and distribution for alternative filmmakers. The existence of "establishment" channels for funding and exhibition, such as the BFI and Channel 4, as well as the output of various filmmaking collectives (such as Retake Film and Video Collective, or the British Audio Film Collective) suggests a vibrant and growing arena well capable of sustaining the amazing output of 1986, which brought us such works as *Playing Away, The Passion of Remembrance,* and *Handsworth Songs.* Moreover, Salman Rushdie's article on *Handsworth Songs* in the *Guardian*—and the ensuing debate—seems from the American vantage point an extraordinary testimony to the importance attached to alternative black films even in "establishment" circles.

The advertisement for the UCLA program describes it as "a rare opportunity for an American audience to discover the wealth of vital and innovative work being done by black British filmmakers, and to gain insight into the political and cultural struggles and achievements taking place in the U.K." Yet it must be said that for most black Americans, seeing black American independent films, or indeed *any* "independent" films, is a "rare opportunity." Despite what seems a relatively greater level of public access in Britain, the major issue on both sides of the Atlantic seems to be, finally, *money*—the lack thereof—both for production-funding and distribution. Better-funded productions—films with high, "slick" production values—get wider distribution, having the right "look," and in their turn tend to make enough money to produce offspring, successors, imitators—in short, to create audience demand, and a tradition of films about issues of interest to black people. So, as in all other things, questions of political power and ideological control arise as soon as one begins discussing "black independent film."

But before I begin to contrast American and British alternative films, I should like to voice at the outset my objections to the unrigorous term "black independent film" itself (even as I am forced at times to use it). It is, like the term "Third World," a conglomeration of compromises which, by the time it is bundled up into a neat phrase, loses most of its intended charge and often comes across merely as a condescending euphemism for what is really going on. The term seems custom-made to cover-up the "questions of political power and ideological control" I just mentioned. It invents some people who just happen to be black and who just happen to have declared some putative artistic and/or financial independence. But artists who have had the term "black independent" applied to them know how little truth there is in that version of things. It seems to me that this conference has so far been engaged in both a conscious and an unconscious interrogation of the term "black independent" itself, so I won't deviate from this subject.

"Black"

In the first place, what is "black"? I was at a program on "black independent woman filmmakers" at New York's Whitney Museum almost exactly a year ago in which a well-known East Indian filmmaker stood up and proclaimed that she, too, was "black," and hence, her work should also have been given recognition. She caused an immediate uproar among many of the filmmakers there. There has been a certain over-mystification and over-specification of "blackness" that has reached the point where some critics and even filmmakers suggest that a "black aesthetic" makes films by blacks as visually distinctive a form as say, traditional black music is from white classical music. I doubt whether such an aesthetic exists, but even if it did, the resulting taxonomy—while perhaps useful for film critics and historians—would do little to address the vexing ideological and political issues that anyone confronts along the axis "non-white."

Our current "essentialist" definitions of "blackness" only share the shortcomings of the essentialist ideology of "whiteness" that has underpinned the course of post-Enlightenment Western history. As a negation of "whiteness," the terms "black" or "non-white," for better or worse, share in its insistent essentialism. "Whiteness" and "blackness" lie perpetually at the intersection of *power* and *metaphor*. Certainly skin color is historical, being a collective sign of the outcome of certain economic and material oppressions and power struggles—events whose results are still very much with us. Yet color equally invokes (particularly in a visual medium such as film) certain *metaphorical* chains (white/black, light/darkness, sun/soil, good/evil, purity/pollution, feeling/thought, and so on). These chains have most often been used by whites against non-whites, and I believe that no effective political alignment can presume to ignore them. It is as useless to rely upon purely ethnic, anthropological, or sociological definitions as it is to insist upon an essentialist definition of skin color; white power has triumphed, after all, as a historical, economic, and finally a *conceptual* form of oppression and hence must be combated on these levels of its operation—and more.

Yet the shortcomings of the too narrow definition of the term

123

"black" are everywhere obvious. The fixation upon racial or even ethnic pedigree has tended to separate American blacks from British blacks, American blacks from West Indian blacks, American blacks from Chinese- and Japanese-Americans, American blacks from Hispanic and Latino-Americans, not to mention American blacks from British Indians and Asians. In America, the chief terminological question remains: does "black" cover Latinos, Asians, Native Americans, and others, or does it just refer to a particular people rooted in the specificity of a particular problematic of slavery, antebellum and post-bellum economic and sexual exploitation, and the 20th Century's characteristic cycles of protest, repression, and assimilation? The question of "immigration" and being "first-" or "second-generation" British is not immediately understandable to black American audiences, since indeed for most of us the problem is not the brevity of our sojourn in American, but its unrelenting and unrelieved length.

In Britain, I would imagine that blacks and Asians share similar problems of immigration and assimilation and are more likely to be talking about the same kinds of confrontations with English society—though here, too, there will be important divergences. *Handsworth Songs,* for all its virtues, lacks a theory of non-white solidarity or interaction. *The Passion of Remembrance,* for all its self-reflexivity, does not directly deal with the ethnic differences *within* the black British community: we never learn what are the affinities and tensions between British-Caribbeans and British-Africans, for instance. A broad-based, even militant, usage of the term "black" as a unifying metaphor is a fitting counter to the pervasive use of "white"—from Lebanon to Lapland—as an object of cultural identification and ideological bonding. Yet certainly there is also much to be said for preserving the specificity of a historical experience—indeed, honest filmmaking requires no less.

Stephen Frears's *My Beautiful Laundrette* (1985) (screenplay by Hanif Kureishi), for all of its critical success among a small white American audience, was entirely ignored by most of the black press (with the exception of David Nicholson's *Black Film Review* in Washington, D.C.), because it was—incorrectly, I think—perceived as being irrelevant to the black American experience. Not incidentally it is simply a fact that all classes and colors in the U.S. tend to associate any accent that sounds vaguely "English" (this includes Irish, Australians, and all classes and varieties of British accents) with a vague signified of "privilege" and "superiority." Therefore, it seems both incongruous and even a bit off-putting for blacks to see other black people on screen speaking in British accents, of whatever variety or stripe. Probably the most important window on black Britain for American blacks has been musical, rather than filmic (or both, in the example of music videos of black British rock groups, which are shown quite frequently on the black-owned cable station Black Entertainment Television) with British reggae and groups such as "Club Nouveau" opening up a black British world of which many black Americans simply were unaware.

But ultimately, a narrow usage of the term "black" is divisive where what is now needed is the forging of new alliances and audiences, and, as I have said, it omits the entire question of an oppressive polity. The fact is, by the term "black," we are speaking of white privilege and the lack thereof. What we might really begin discussing here, then, is the existence of *insurgent* or *alternative* cinemas, without mystifying the color of its producers. Such cinemas would be open to an entire host of adversarial groups and concerns, and, as is beginning to happen in America, articulate feminist and gay issues, as well as the experiences of various non-white filmmakers.

"Independent"

Secondly, we must ask: what is really an "independent film"? Anyone who has made even the simplest super 8 film knows that that phrase is a contradiction in terms. No filmmaker is independent in the way that, say, a poet is. Filmmaking, both capital- and labor-intensive, is the *most* dependent art form. This is both the blessing and curse of the form. So the question has never been one of "dependence" or "independence," but merely the nature of one's dependence. At least in the U.S., filmmaking, more than other art forms, operates under Keynesian, or demand-side, economic constraints. Rather than a film being able to seek and find an audience once made, many films without well-defined markets may simply not get funding in the first place.

Once more, then, we are dealing with a question of *reception,* but in this case, reception can even pre-empt or censor the actual production. The questions remain, then: what kinds of statements and images will a society tolerate, and where will it tolerate them, and with what frequency? Hence, you cannot easily see films by black filmmakers in America, period—British or American, dependent or independent.

At best, non-white films, by a kind of Marcusian "repressive toler-ance" become safe totems, tabooed because they ventilate so many of society's own taboos. They say the embarrassing, the unsayable. To some extent, of course, any truthful and articulate black person—whether politician, writer, dancer, actor, or filmmaker—is bound to upset the status quo, because, at least in America, his or her very *presence* is an implicit taboo or embarrassment, reminding anyone who choses to be reminded of America's prior and enduring oppression and exploitation of blacks. All too often, independent films are packed away for discrete presentation of elite museums, late-night educational television programs, and infrequent, often poorly attended confer-ences on "independent cinema."

Interestingly, the independent film community itself encourages a kind of subtle racism: it is generally assumed that if a white filmmaker's film is "independent" (i.e., under-funded or under-produced), then it may be characterized by some alleged violation of Classic Realist style, a trait that is judged, depending on the critic, "experimentalist," "Godardian," "amateurish." Yet the almost universal assumption that high production values are the premise of good filmmaking tends to work against blacks more forcefully than against whites. A white film may be coded "independent" and rated critically often on the sole basis of technique, regardless of content. Sloppy filmmaking can be read as auteurist brilliance. Yet if a black filmmaker's film is "indepen-dent" it is often seen to have been a result of the film's "content": technical issues are overlooked, even where—as is often the case—they are an intrinsic part of the filmmaker's message. Black filmmakers are seen as furnishing, at best, documentary or raw sociological data. It is considered that the film is good *despite* its technique, not *because of* what I call "visual recodings" of old stereotyped images of black skin on screen. Even the most successful independent black independent films (such as Spike Lee's *She's Gotta Have It*) have fallen victim to this critical blindness. The reception of these films has usually split along the form/content dichotomy, with their considerable formal innovations being—as in much early criticism of black novels and poetry—sold short for easy sociological discussions of content.

The Difference

Finally, black American and British filmmakers seem to be asking different questions about the whole issue of *assimilation*. For black American filmmakers, the question is not so much "what would it mean to assimilate?" or "what is my relation to American-ness?" These questions were settled, mainly in the negative, long ago. To some extent, the black American independent films I have seen are preoccupied with the question "how can I best *keep from* becoming like white Americans? How can I fulfill my personal aspirations and yet best preserve my distinctness, my 'grooviness' in the stultifyingly square American context?" For black American filmmakers, an "American" identity as such no longer has anything to offer—if it ever did: indeed, the entire history of blacks in America has been the history of whites *taking from*, rather than *giving to* blacks in America (culturally, economically, spiritually).

If we were to invent an "average" black independent film on either side of the Atlantic, we would find that in America, racism and racial politics, at least in terms of mainstream film imagery, are very much caught up in different conceptual structures than in Britain. The black remains a former slave who has moved (not emigrated) to an urban setting from a predominantly rural setting—both terrains are present in the same continental land mass and are effectively available for filmmakers to exploit as their fictional stage. For specific, historical reasons, the roles of "mammy" (the urban or Southern domestic maid), Uncle Tom (the "house nigger," household retainer, and quiet collaborator), the black buck (the "bad nigger," unregenerate, sexy, violent), as well as the agrarian or rural peasant worker still hover over almost every mass cultural depiction of blacks like unquiet ghosts, and even inhabit the works of black filmmakers who are trying their best to

127

undermine them. Such paradigms do not play a role in the black British films I have seen. They have other concerns.

Furthermore, black American filmmakers, for all their savvy about street ways and city life, still represent the urban landscape as if it were a hostile territory, and often, it is. This tendency, coupled with a recurrent nostalgia for "Africa," however defined, tends to project an "other place," a place of deliverance or redemption which is always the potential opposite or counterpart of the urban conditions represented.

In America, "black independent films" (for want of a better term) fit into three broad groups: what I call "blacks framed in their place"—films that depict the racist past, or its legacy (paradigmatic limitation); films that show blacks fighting, with only measured success, the white assumptions of black inferiority that code them into place, and that would freeze the status quo; and finally, films that try, through the film medium itself to achieve what I call "recoding" through the use of the film medium itself (syntagmatic freedom). It is these latter, formally "experimental" films, whose technique is largely dismissed as "sloppy," or "low budget" filmmaking.

Finally it seems to me that in black British films the analysis of the "structural" crisis of late Western capitalism is better, more rigorous, in British films, perhaps because these conditions are closer, more concentrated here, and also because of Britain's better developed tradition of social criticism and political and economic analysis in films.

Incitements

I look forward to the day when such questions as we have taken up here may find resonance in diverse settings of reception. In order to nurture the fledgling Black Cinema Movements on both sides of the Atlantic, demand must be stimulated, audiences consolidated, the channels of reception widened. Specifically, mainstream newspapers (such as the *Guardian,* and, to an extent the *New York Times*) must continue to discern in the new black cinema a significant new direction in the history of film, and encourage wider debates on the challenging voices that emerge from these works. Visual media will need to increase mass-cultural outlets for films with unconventional themes and opinions. Overall, we need to rethink a "star" system based on narrow narcissistic identifications by white audiences, a system that tends to discount in advance films with largely unknown black actors (even *She's Gotta Have It* had to be sold as "Spike Lee's Film," with Lee marketed as "the black Woody Allen," in order to furnish the "hook," or introductory appeal, for the film). Finally, we must remedy the monopoly in black cinema studies of a few books, mostly written over a decade ago: Edward Mapp's *Blacks in American Films: Today and Yesterday* (Metuchen: Scarecrow Press, 1972); Donald Bogle's *Toms, Coons, Mulattoes, Mammies, and Bucks: An Interpretive History of Blacks in American Films* (New York: Viking, 1973); Daniel Leab's *From Sambo to Superspade: The Black Experience in Motion Pictures* (Boston: Houghton Mifflin, 1975); James P. Murray's *To Find an Image: Blacks in Films from Uncle Tom to Superfly* (Indianapolis: Bobbs Merrill, 1973); Gary Null's *Black Hollywood* (Secaucus: Citadel Press, 1975); Thomas Cripps's *Slow Fade to Black* (New York: Oxford University Press, 1977) and *Black Film as Genre* (Bloomington: Indiana University Press, 1978). There is not yet a thorough "history" of British and/or American black independent filmmakers in the U.S., and even the above books, for all their merits, largely misunderstood the developments of the seventies and totally missed those of the eighties. Without getting caught in the trap of applying elitist terminology to presumably anti-elitist works for non-academic audiences, we must promote critically sophisticated chronicles of the extraordinary ferment in black cinematic expression that—against formidable economic and political odds—the last decade has raised.

10

Mass Visual Productions

My starting premise will be that our mass culture in America today consists of an entirely new set of artifacts—mass visual productions. These new artifacts require new ways of seeing and new ways of thinking about what we are seeing. It never has been enough to just see a film—and now, more than ever, we need, not just to "see," but to "see through" what we see on screen. This is a crucial distinction to remember: the difference between "seeing" what's on screen and "seeing through" what's on screen. In the first part of my talk, I shall look at some of the properties and tendencies of film as a mass medium. Later, I will look at some categories which will be useful in discussing images of black people in white films.

We need to learn how to read visual media more carefully nowadays because we are increasingly surrounded by them. Between the 19th and 20th Centuries, the environment of European and American societies changed to one dominated largely by mass-produced consumer and media products. Previously, our environment consisted of natural objects, or human transformations of natural objects—houses, furniture, clothing. Most of the world, including most African and third world cultures, still has an environment that consists of natural products, or artifacts created from natural products. But in the 20th Century, European and American technology have created mass-media and consumer goods, man-made goods that have a weight equal to or often greater than that of nature and natural objects. Our environment has changed and, therefore, our ways of seeing have to change. These mass-produced artifacts have an enormous social and psychological impact on all of us.

Today I wish to speak about the impact of such mass-productions upon an audience's beliefs and actions, especially the way these mass-produced images have political, ideological, and psychological effects. Those of you with children should be especially concerned about the possible psychological effects of these images.

The main kinds of mass-produced images that concern us today are motion picture films and television films, although there are other kinds of visual images that one could talk about: there are billboards, there are magazine advertisements, there are television advertisements, there are movie advertisements, and so on. Today I shall focus on feature films.

Let's ask a couple of very elemental questions about film. First of all, what is a film? This may seem like a simple place to begin, but I think in this kind of study, we want to begin at the most fundamental starting point. The experience of a film duplicates our everyday experience of reality. In a film, the objects on the screen have been recorded and played back, just as our memories record everyday reality and then recognize it whenever they encounter the same objects again. Our belief in photography, and especially motion picture photography, is our belief that on some level, everything that happens on the screen has first happened in front of a camera. We are to the screen as the camera lens was to reality. We suspend our disbelief concerning what the film unfolds. In viewing a film, we temporarily forget that we are seeing a strip of edited photos being mechanically sped past a projector at 24 frames per second. We do not actually have any proof about what has been photographed, or of the conditions and demands under which it was photographed.

In the film experience, a dead strip of film lives for us as an audience when it is magnified and illuminated and projected onto a screen. A film is never "just the same again," but always something much larger, much more. The magnification of the film image makes it into a public and not a private event. The reactions of the other spectators in the audience give us a strong feeling of a "reality" that our group ratifies, the group to which we belong because we recognize, as do the other members of the audience, what happens on screen as being real. We belong to a group that recognizes the screen images as something that it has seen before. We see the events on screen as events that concern us. Therefore, as I said before, film is a *social and political* statement about the nature of things—political, because it involves issues of mass belief and mass understanding. If a viewer gets the same message as his or her neighbor, then they hereby constitute a group that belongs together, linked by understanding. (Anyone who has ever watched a Woody Allen film, say in the South, or in Germany, will notice that there may be ten people out of two hundred who laugh at certain moments—because they're getting the joke.) So one thing reacting in a certain way does in this kind of audience environment is to define us as being either in a particular group or outside of a particular group. Your response to a film defines you as being either in the know or out of the know.

In the early days of film, most images were not actually "mass"— they were viewed with primitive private viewing instruments such as Edison's "Kinetoscope" (1895) in nickelodeons. Thus we would speak not of "mass," but of many individuals screening films separately. Perhaps with the arrival of the VCR, we are returning to an era of isolated, private viewings. But in any case, the dynamics of watching a film involve investing the screen with a certain amount of belief, belief that one also believes that others hold. We are inclined to believe that film expresses a general belief, a general notion of truth. What happens on film is not just "true to me," or "true in my experience," or "one person's experience," but also comes to be seen as *generally* true, or "what everybody knows is true." The camera, it seems, shrinks and records a prior reality to a film strip, and the projector enlarges and re-presents that reality, so that the right viewers can identify it in the right way.

But although the camera may be a "true" observer, a camera does not give us everything. In fact, a camera distorts reality. Many film theoreticians argue that it is this distortion that makes film an art form and not just a mere mechanical means of reproduction. The film director makes us not merely spectators, but *ideal* spectators—by cutting (montage), production, and various forms of post-production. A film always *selects* what is put before the camera, and later, the projector. This is its great virtue. You never get the whole truth, you get a selection of the truth. The camera doesn't lie. And it also doesn't tell the truth. All it does it tell the story. The question is: do we believe the story that it tells? We would like to believe it, because we would like to satisfy our need to hear a story told, but this issue of belief has very little to do with the logic or factuality of the story. For now, then, let us define a "film" as "a series of recorded and repeatable moving images that aims to make a viewer believe in the story or reality it claims to portray." The word "claim" is important here, as we shall see later.

Now what does it mean for a viewer to "believe" in a film? Clearly one believes what one expects to believe or what one is prepared to believe. From its earliest days, audiences realized that films could convey both absolute reality and absolute fantasy. Nothing keeps film from portraying real, believable experiences. We have the phrases "seeing is believing," and in film we can "see" what "really happened" and preserve it forever as documentary history. Yet film can also, governed by a filmmaker's will, imagination, and ideological slant, present a fantasy or ideal world that has nothing to do with the real world, but present it *as if it were the real world*. So a film can either record the real world exactly or it can present a fantasy world, but the conditions are the same: we still think that it is the real world that we are looking at. So these two poles—fantasy on the one hand, and recording on the other hand—have always co-existed as antithetical tendencies since the beginning of the film art. (As in the contrast between Georges Méliès and the Lumière brothers, French filmmakers in the late 19th Century. Méliès, a magician, devoted himself to exploiting cinema as a medium for fantasy. The Lumières aimed to show viewers everyday events: factory scenes, trains entering stations, etc.)

Because we wish to believe in film from the very first frames, and because films can portray both fantasy and history, there is the danger that our wish to believe will be misused by a filmmaker who wishes us to believe certain things. When confronting any mass-produced image, we must ask "does this image claim to portray history, or fantasy, and what are the differences between the claims and what is really being shown?" We shall see in *Birth of a Nation* the difference between the claim for historical accuracy and the actual image is great indeed.

The difference between film as fantasy and film as recorded history should be clear, but it is not always so. The only way one could probably have a completely historical film would be to invent an all-seeing camera that would record all angles of a particular historical event. If we could possibly see the thousands of miles of film that would result, then we might really have something that would be a "historical" recording. In fact, such a use of film has been attempted in Andy Warhol's *Empire* (1965), which gives us a single view of the Empire State Building for twenty-four hours, dusk to dawn. In fact, all normal films deviate from this "recording" ideal. Film, like all art forms, is selective, but the more selective the film, the more it is able to disguise distortion under the mask of exact reproduction. Michelangelo cuts out just the right amount of marble to make a beautiful sculpture. Cutting and selection are properties of any cultural text or image, but they allow it to be used for all sorts of psychological and sociological mischief.

Let me summarize what I have said up to now. First of all, that we are increasingly inundated by man-made visual artifacts that elevate themselves as a privileged kind of truth, photographic truth, which can seem as believable as (and often more believable than) reality itself. Secondly, film can accurately record everyday events, but is much more likely to serve as a selection of those events, tending in the hands of skilled filmmakers either towards accuracy or distortion. The third element here is the notion of belief: do you believe it? Does an audience believe that this distortion is truly reality?

Some films that claim to portray history actually portray fantasies, and some films that claim to portray fantasies are actually (often indirectly) portraying historical truths. The films I have chosen today fit these categories. *King Kong,* presumably an imaginary voyage in search of a giant ape in darkest Africa, actually gives a fairly accurate portrayal of the mercenary mentality that led white men to kidnap, not giant apes, but millions of black people, from Africa. *King Kong,* perhaps unintentionally, is an allegory of the slave trade. It re-enacts (even in a certain historical sense) the actions and motives of the first slave-traders and colonialists whose main ambition was to plunder Africa of its natural riches and human resources. But this white attack on black people here is masked by a reversal—we seem to see a black attack on white womanhood, in the person of Fay Wray. Hence, the film is "historical" in revealing (again unintentionally) much about the various sexual fantasies and phobias of its makers—and also those of many of its viewers. Moreover, *King Kong* gives very good insights into how so-called documentaries of "African expeditions" in the twenties, thirties, and forties were made and then shown in this country and elsewhere under the pretext of reporting "the way things are" in exotic lands. Notice that the cameraman has a very prominent role on this expedition. He is quite careful to crank out—in true newsreel-documentary style—a film of each step in the expedition's incursion into Africa. If the black man is coded here as the "man with the spear," the white man here is "the man with the camera."

Notice particularly in this clip how the whites always behave as individuals, while the blacks are always seen (except for the chief) as group phenomena. Also look at the way Africans are coded by highly obvious external clues (Afro wigs, bones, paints, etc.) that quickly signify "blackness = native."

As you can see, *King Kong*, while calling itself "fantasy," actually acts out some of the same psychosexual phobias of the white male that we shall be seeing in a so-called "historical" film, *Birth of a Nation*. In other words, while the "pretexts" of the films are completely different, the "subtexts" (the desire of the black male for the white woman, the general debasement and primitiveness of black behavior and culture) remain the same. So the denoted/explicit message here is fantasy, but the connoted codes are meant to give the viewer a real image of the "reality" of the black mind (after all, these are real black extras, aren't they? . . . straight from Watts . . . actually, the black here encodes a more general connotation of "the savage"—note the completely "un-African" *leis* on the sacrificial maiden, straight out of a Polynesian film . . . also notice that the music is essentially stolen from American Indian, not African rhythms . . . also interesting is that, due to some mix-up, or shortage of extras, the gorilla dance is being performed by *whites!*) A terrible waste of talent for Rex Ingram, first black to earn a Phi Beta Kappa key at Northwestern University, and a graduate of that university's medical school in 1919. This is the kind of work that was available to one of the finest black actors of his generation in 1933.

There were similar films to *King Kong* in the early history of Hollywood. There was a film made in 1914 called *African Natives*. Another was called *Theodore Roosevelt's Camp in Africa*. These were supposed to be documentary photographic versions of what actually happened. But in fact, these so-called "documentary" films were lies: they had nothing to do with Africa, and were actually filmed here, in Hollywood—the *King Kong* set was erected a short distance away. So these early films relied on a viewer's willingness to supplement his or her faulty knowledge of other lands or other ethnic groups with a cinematic "quick fix." We were told what we didn't know very quickly, in an easily palatable form. We had films in the 1890s such as Edison's *Watermelon Contest* (blacks eating watermelon: something that whites probably would not have seen, but when they saw it in the film, it became fact), or another one called *A West Indian Woman Bathing a Baby* (that's just what it is: about three minutes long, and about a West Indian woman bathing a baby—but again, this was newsworthy: you can witness an exotic spectacle as if you were there). Motion pictures have always tried to take call upon this "recording" aspect of film—to take advantage of the way we would like to believe that a film is an accurate recording of what actually happened. The new technology of film photography reinforced this false claim—in the manner of other films whose technological brilliance and innovations have hidden the reactionary nature of their ideological messages. I believe that *Birth of a Nation* is in this category—you would like to believe that *Birth of a Nation* is true, because it does what it does so well (montages, cutting, camera angles); or even the *Star Wars* films (encoding of the main villains as black men from head to toe): we would like to believe that that film is true, because it is so enjoyable to watch, so technologically brilliant. The viewer sees these films and says "this is how it is," or worse, "that's how *they* are." One always has to be careful that a

20. *A West Indian Woman Bathing a Baby.* An early Edison short (1895).

technologically well-produced film does not seem believable because it is technologically slick (*The Color Purple* vs. independent films).

One standard method for cloaking the destructiveness of black portrayals in film, then, is to simply call them "history" or "documentation" . . . a device we have seen ever since the like of *Theodore Roosevelt's Camp in Africa.* Now I want to talk about history and its relationship to film.

History. Film exists to tell a kind of replacement history—even the most preposterous western on some level purports to tell the "history" of Western settlement. Warfare, colonization, scientific and geographical discovery, victory over the forces of evil: these are the archetypes of American film, and each of them has an implicit historical field of reference.

History, in the European and American mind, was made by whites. Blacks remain more or less the same, untouched by the passage of time. Particularly in the early days of filmmaking, the black was conceived of as changeless. Blacks had certain roles: stooges, retainers (maids, butlers), brutes, dancers, thieves, child-like—because they *were* a certain way. Enduring, immune to education or other betterment, blacks could be excluded from dynamic possibilities of the filmed American Dream ("rags to riches"—upward mobility), and remain unimprovable, static, and timeless. Many white viewers recognize in this stable, immune, enduring black a fixed place of authority. In others words, in order for whites always to have a certain authority over blacks, blacks always have to be the same thing. This is extremely important: one never sees these stereotypes change, because if they changed, whites' view of themselves would have to change. In a sense, the films say nothing at all about blacks, but say a lot about the person who would enjoy making or viewing such a film. The message of black inferiority is addressed to a viewer who wishes to believe in white superiority. The viewer sees the stereotype and says: "Yes, I know this is how they really are, therefore I am better."

The history that whites have made, on screen and off, empties black skin of any historical or material reference, except as former slaves. The notion of the eternal black "character" is invented to justify the enforced economic disadvantage that we enjoy (or don't enjoy) in this society. In films from King Vidor's 1929 *Hallelujah!* through Spielberg's 1985 *The Color Purple,* blacks' behavior is portrayed as being unrelated to the history that whites have trapped them in. Let me repeat: that behavior is being portrayed as something static, enduring, and unchangeable, unrelated to the history that whites have trapped them in. Blacks are seen as ahistorical. The African films corroborate this notion. In the notorious African films—say *Tarzan's Peril* (1951), or *King Kong* (1933)—we can see that even before slavery, Africans have always acted the way they do in America . . . therefore three hundred years of slavery and oppression made no difference! They must be that way by nature, because they were that way in Africa!

So the history of black film stereotypes is the history of the denial of history in favor of an artificially constructed general truth about the unchanging black "character." We are being taken out of history into the realm of myth: things which never change, which were so at the beginning, are so now, and ever shall be. We would all like to believe that things have gotten better since *Birth of a Nation,* but I have to report that the progress is very small. The problem is that, for reasons mentioned above, stereotypes never completely disappear. Because film is infinitely repeatable, and it records and preserves images, that film will never change, and because viewers see that film as denoting an unchanging truth about blacks, they will *always be able to believe in that image.* The nature of stereotypes is to insulate themselves from historical change, or from counter-examples in the real world. Caricatures breed more caricatures, or metamorphose into more harmless forms, or simply repeat, but they are still with us. Aunt Jemima, conceived as an ad campaign in 1932—shortly before the film based on a similar character, *Imitation of Life,* appeared—still sits on the pancake box. Similarly, demeaning films still are shown and re-shown, and believed in, and have already been conditioned by millions of reels to accept these mythologies of blackness as the "real truth," despite any subsequent positive images. Negative images, as in *The Jewel of the Nile, Taxi Driver,* and many Clint Eastwood or Charles Bronson films, continue to be made.

Now let us consider the relationship between propaganda films and films that pretend to be "historical." A film becomes "propaganda" and no longer merely "fiction" when its aim is to introduce or reinforce a set of political power relationships between social groups, and for our purposes, we can talk about the relationships between blacks and whites. *Birth of a Nation,* as we shall see, is neither the historical document it claims to be, nor a harmless fictional entertainment, but something more dangerous than either.

But even within the realms of fantasy and propaganda, there are various possibilities of belief. There are believable fantasy films (say, the *Star Wars* films) and unbelievable fantasy films (today, the "Buck Rogers" series). Belief depends on the expectations and experience of an audience. Similarly, there is believable and unbelievable propaganda. Hitler's propaganda minister, Joseph Goebbels, in the thirties produced a virulently anti-Semitic film entitled *Jud Süss,* about how Jews supposedly infiltrated and took over the city of Stuttgart in prior times, with the leading villain, a Mr. Oppenheimer, raping a young

German girl, who later commits suicide because of the shame involved. The "Jew," as the lynch mobs constantly refer to him, is finally hanged, not for his various state and civil "crimes," but for mixing the races. Sound familiar? The opening titles of the film make the claim to historical truth, just as *Birth of a Nation* does, even more brilliantly: "the events depicted in this film are based on historical fact." After this film was distributed, Goebbels found that he had to re-shoot large parts of it because even a pre-war German audience, well-prepared for anti-Semitic plots and Jew-baiting, still found it incredible. On the other hand, *Triumph of the Will,* which we shall view part of in a minute, was taken not as a skillful manipulation of an already mass-spectacle, but as the historical record of the Nuremberg Nazi Party rally of 1934.

Today the differences between fantasy and history are rarely so clear-cut. Indeed, most mass-images in our culture come to us as "in-between" artifacts. Advertising, films, and television images establish role-, behavior-, and relationship-models that are, through their repetition, even more effective on an unconscious level than rhetorical propaganda on a conscious level. Modern media images do not claim to be historical or actual "truth," but at the same time, they have a "mythifying" and "exemplary" impact that gives them a value somewhat higher than truth. They present, not verifiable facts, but implicit models of belief and action.

How are these models constructed? They become what I will call "codes." Stereotypes ultimately connect to form larger complexes of symbols and connotations. These codes then begin to form a kind of "private conversation" among themselves without needing to refer back to the real world for their facticity. The pleasure of recognizing codes displaces the necessity for a viewer to verify them. Since many mass-media images today claim to be neither reality nor fantasy (witness the docu-drama), there are no useful criteria by which to inspect or challenge the claims to truth that these visual images and events constantly make. One merely recognizes and repeats them. To object that a particular portrayal or stereotyped code is a distortion brings the response: "It's not reality; it's fantasy," while to claim that the particular film is unbelievable because of its stereotypes brings the

141

response "Then why is the film so popular? If so many people recognize this experience/code/type, then it must be real"—a classic double-bind case.

We have to be ready, as film-goers, not only to see films, but also to see through them; we have to be willing to figure out what the film is claiming to portray, and also to scrutinize what the film is actually showing. Finally, we need to ask from whose social vantage point any film becomes credible or comforting, and ask why. Indeed, racism in the cinema might be described as the tendency to recycle certain ethnic codes, already familiar to a series of privileged viewers, in order to reinforce their familiarity, despite the changes that may have gone on in the real world.

The coding of blacks in film, as in the wider society, involves a history of images and signs associating black skin color with servile behavior and marginal status. While these depictions may have reflected prior economic oppression of blacks, they also tended to perpetuate it. Through the exact repetition which is film's main virtue, these associations became part of film's typological vocabulary.

But remember that I said that in any system of codes there are several representations made at the same time. "Codes" are not singular portrayals of one thing or another, but larger, complex relationships. Hence, American films, especially, have always featured not merely images of blacks, but implicit or explicit co-relations between the debasement of blacks and the elevation and mythification of whites. So for a white audience to accept largely unbelievable stereotypes about black inferiority implied a belief in the contrasting position of superiority the white hero achieved. In some ways, then, defamatory racial caricatures, infinitely repeatable in filmic form, allow those white viewers who believe in them to place themselves in a position of stable and unchanging superiority with respect to blacks. The cinematic stereotype functions by feeding back susceptible white viewers the way they see (and wish to be seen by) a given minority culture. A brief list of such stereotypes in American films would include the stooge/jester, the buck/brute, the tragic mulatto, the body-servant/mammy/house-maid, and the loyal sidekick/retainer. Notice that whereas each of these roles has a different connotation in terms of type of work,

142

intelligence, and psychology, all of them are coded with regard to whatever whites they encounter (they have become fixed stereo-types)—they all represent inferiority, powerlessness, and marginality. Seeming variety really is social fixity and limitation. Indeed, these figures exist only as potential contrasts to white figures—like a black-board against which the white characters stand out all the more clearly.

To end my lecture, I would like to name three tactics through which racial stereotypes are forged and perpetuated in all periods of Hollywood film (especially pre-World War II films). Whenever you see blacks in Hollywood movies especially, you should be looking for three kinds of operation: mythification; marking; and omission.

First, *mythification*. The magnification of the film image also involves a kind of enlargement of what it portrays. We "look up to" films, literally, and screen events rapidly become "larger than life." Through repetition and apparent realism, they soon replace life, existing along-side what we know from our everyday lives. Film is never "one person's story"—film is always typical, broadcasting certain codes about social status and interrelationships. Mythification can both elevate and de-grade. Indeed, the two properties are interdependent. The same film language that magnifies white heroes reduces black people. Bette Davis needs Hattie McDaniel, and white male heroes need faithful male servants. White women need black maids to make them seem more womanly; white men need black butlers or sidekicks to make them seem more manly. Soon, by mythification and repetition, filmed images become models, positive or negative, for behavior, describing structures, limits, and an overall repertoire from which viewers in the real world select their actions and opinions.

Even in the first few minutes of the Nazi propaganda film, *Triumph of the Will*, we have a classic example of mythification at work. *King Kong* proported to be a fantasy, but this film proports to be a "document," a historical recording, simple, true, and immediate. Instead, it is a lesson in repetition, and the relationship of repetition to propagandistic mythification. The repeated gestures—the gaze and the Gruss—are simple, but they encode complex psychological issues involving willed dominance and subordination. We see in the first few moments not only a mass-spectacle orchestrated specifically in order to make a gigantic statement, but we also watch the spectacle being watched and participated in by the crowds that form upon Hitler's arrival. The mutual entwinement of Hitler and his so-called "people" or "Volk" is encoded in the way the crowd watches Hitler watching them. The "chaos" of the mass group is given "order" by Hitler's empty gaze. As is the case in the interaction of film and audience, the observer finds his or her meaning and identity in his or her ability to recognize— and be recognized by—the "star" out there upon which he or she gazes. Hitler's stare gives them the sense that their stares have been answered and legitimated. The mutual confirmation of this gazing is coded by the repetition and imitation of the "Hitler Gruss," which, again, Hitler performs and they repeat. Similarly, part of the fascination and danger of film is that it offers us large-scale gestures that we feel make us important, once we repeat them. (By how many impressionable viewers will the lesbian scene in *Color Purple* be repeated?—in the case of John Hinckley and Martin Scorsese's *Taxi Driver,* the impressionable and unbalanced can imitate mass gestures offered to them by Hollywood productions, often with very real and horrifying, actions.) Instead of *Triumph of the Will,* the film should be called "failure of the will" or at least the triumph of Hitler's will over the crowd . . . but in fact, one of the points of the film is to show that the two wills have become inseparable—and indeed, the movie viewer is caught in the mutual recognition and imitation . . . we watch the watcher (Hitler) being watched (by the crowd).

If you take the spectacle of Hitler's arrival as a symbol for mass-spectacles of every sort, you can exactly see the source of their power: mythification teaches us the joy of imitating the behavior and gestures of significant others with whose power (note the cross-cuts to lines of soldiers) and tenderness (Hitler with mothers and babies) and age (cross-cuts to ancient architecture and fountains) we can share a narcissistic identity. We often watch and identify with movie stars on screen (and pursue them in person) in the same ways. Being seen, recognized, and acknowledged by them confirms our identities. One might term the black in Hollywood film the one always in search of the confirming, empowering white glance, but the one whose glance only confirms

21. *Triumph of the Will.* The Nuremberg Rally.

the white's position of power, because it remains averted, directed towards the ground or the sky.

The next tactic after *mythification* is *marking.* "Marking" the black allows the viewer to "register" the image. "Marking" is necessary because the state of "blackness" or being "colored" in fact cannot be strictly defined. At best, white Americans have always had difficulty defining "Negro" or "colored" (and indirectly, themselves, since their "essence" has always been tantamount to being "not-colored" or "not-negro"). The terms of racial identity—"white" and "black"—denote not any one thing, but a whole range of possibilities, all defined, not positively by being this or that, but negatively, by *not* being "white." The needs of image-making rhetoric, then, require black skin to be marked as being as black as possible to eliminate any ambiguity. The dramatic contrast of light and dark, in general, is indispensable to the photographic image. Hence, the Hollywood black had to be made up to seem very black, as in the case of early films where whites wore blackface to seem as black as possible. When black actors and actresses began to assume the roles of blacks, the studios required them also (Bert Williams, Nina Mae McKinney, Fredi Washington, and Lena Horne are only a few examples) to darken their skins. The contrast of black and white assists the use of the color black for stereotypical and ideological purposes, hence we find domestics, jazz musicians, and others wearing white articles of clothing. Often, this contrast becomes a symbol as well for the metaphysical conflict between good and evil, as in the dark horses and white horses of cowboy Westerns, and so on. Other kinds of marking involve "Negro dialect" (early films such as *Birth of a Nation* even felt it necessary to write dialect on title cards that came on when blacks were supposed to be speaking!—and Louise Beavers, as well as many other fine black actresses and actors, were required to learn "Negro dialects" before being allowed to speak their roles . . . yet few film-goers would have actually believed that they did not really speak in their cinematic "Negro dialect"!); elevation/ lowness (Mantan Mooreland, Stepin Fetchit, and others, generally shorter than the whites they played next to); motion/stasis . . . physical mobility/social immobility; dependence/independence; distance from center/proximity to center; cleanliness/dirtiness; distinction/group-mass. In all these ways, the black is visually "marked" in the cinematic frame—black skin is real and self-evident (the screen says: "this is a servant, who happens to be black"), but actually encodes a deeper and unspoken social message ("we can expect to see blacks as servants in the real world; blacks are only meant to be servants"). The message is: "here is a black servant." The code is: "blacks make good servants."

Finally, the tactic of *omission* is the most difficult to spot, because it entails seeing what is not there. The first step for understanding any type of propaganda is the ability to observe its omissions. As we have seen, the basic quality of film is to present some things quite accurately while omitting others. *Mythification*, indeed, works by magnifying positive features of a given group or marking and omitting others. Film as an art form says "to see is to know." Therefore the saying goes, "seeing is believing." What you don't know (or see) won't hurt you. But the portrayal of blacks in American cinema has been testimony to the fact that "what we don't see" and "what they don't see" hurts us—precisely because we are what we don't see. The two most important political poles of any film are absence and presence. Note that in *Triumph of the Will,* we see everything about Hitler and the Germans that he leads except what they will forever be infamous for: mass arrests: mass tortures; military aggression and brutality; mass murder. Instead of these negatives, we get the mass images of the well-directed and technically proficient mass rally . . . a virtual spectacle of omitted details. In the final analysis, then, it is not true that we don't see what is not on screen. On the contrary, when the absence is repeated constantly, then we see *that* it is not there. Absence becomes reality. Think about black images that we don't see in *King Kong,* as well as more recent films. We don't see blacks as teachers, thinkers, humanitarians, people who command respect and authority from others. (Norman Jewison's *A Soldier's Story* (1984) gives us a somewhat broader spectrum of black types in Hollywood cinema than we have previously known).

From the earliest days of film, omission was the method of choice in designing and tailoring mass images of black people. Indeed, censorship has been used ever since the film of Jack Johnson defeating his white opponent Tommy Burns in 1908 was taken out of distribution in order to erase potentially positive and strong images of blacks from the public mind. Throughout the thirties and forties, Hollywood films with black stars typically used them in easily removable excerpts, "optional" numbers, or scenes that could be removed for Southern distribution. The omission of the black, then, has meant the presence of the stereotype. The code has not merely meant that black skin was marked in negative ways in contrast to positive white mythologizations. It has also meant that for every dark, ape-like, dull-witted, unintelligent, sexually promiscuous, drug-taking, docile, irresponsible, antisocial, unambitious, and violent black, the entire range of countervailing and antithetical role-types, always available to white actors and actresses, has been (until recently) systematically omitted. What we don't see in these films is us—and that hurts us. See if you can see yourselves in *Birth of a Nation.* You won't, but the film is perhaps interesting because credible on other narrative levels, even to a black viewer. For the white viewer looking to have his/her superiority confirmed by such a film, logical contradiction and historical inaccuracy have mattered little.

Now that we have seen how black images can be degraded and how certain whites can be mythified, let us now look at a film in which we have both degradation and mythification, as well as marking and omission. This film is *Birth of a Nation*, which, like *Triumph of the Will*, pretends to a certain historical accuracy. D.W. Griffith, in this film, insidiously intersperses in the fictional action what he calls "Historical Facsimiles" (depictions of Appomattox, Ford's Theatre, the South Carolina House of Representatives, "the first legislative session under reconstruction"). In the first cases, these reconstructions of reality are based in size and detail upon actual settings or contemporary portraits. In that sense, they are "historical facsimiles." But one is led to believe that the entire film is historical because of the claim that it makes to be a true representation of history. Hence, one viewer claims "this film taught me more history in three hours than in weeks and months of study in the classroom." President Wilson (also a famous American historian), who arranged a screening of the film at the White House, is said to have exclaimed "It's like writing history with lightning!" Well it's not history, though it may be lightning. Although some of the sets—say, of Appomattox and Ford's Theatre—are visually accurate, *Birth of a Nation* (in the manner of its inspiring texts, a novel and play by Thomas Dixon, both called *The Clansman*) portrays blacks eating, taking swigs of whiskey, taking off their shoes—all in the State House of Representatives. By implication then, since part of the film has a simulated history, the entire film seems to share in a certain credibility as history.

But the film, as one reviewer puts it, actually is not history. Rather, it "gambles on the public ignorance of our own history." In a similar fashion, public ignorance of other lands made the exotic newsreel or adventure film (to Africa or to India) possible. The "quick fix" approach to an often unpalatable history continues right through *Gone with the Wind* and even right up to the stereotyped and often derogatory images of third world peoples in the *Indiana Jones* films.

Rather than accurate history, *Birth of a Nation* is really a nightmare

148

vision of the future. It is, in fact, the first "social disaster" movie. Like *Earthquake* or *The Day After*, it re-enacts what never happened, but does so in an attempt to keep it from ever happening. The images of surly and ignorant blacks in power and threatening whites, pushing them off sidewalks, grabbing their possessions, preaching mixed marriages, attempting the rape of a white teenager, flogging loyal blacks—none of this ever really happened: these scenes are no longer history, but anxiety. Freud suggests that we stage our worst fears so as to protect ourselves against them, should they actually come. Certainly *Birth of a Nation* fits this description of an almost neurotic necessity to enact one's own humiliation in order to fictively redress it. Interestingly, since the surly blacks are always white actors in blackface, we can see that the film guarantees its own truth value: blacks were once this way, but have been put down by the KKK for the good of all, enabling this film to be made, using whites now, and not real blacks. The fact that real blacks cannot be used attests to and confirms the truth of the film: they are dangerous, so dangerous that we cannot even let them pretend they are being arrogant towards us. There is a historical irony in the fact that Lillian Gish, who is pushed off a sidewalk in 1915 by blackface actors, actually does get pushed off the sidewalk by a real black actor, Raymond St. Jacques, in the 1967 film *The Comedians*. What kind of progress *that* is is the question we filmgoers must ask ourselves each time we are asked to "sit back, relax, and enjoy the show."

Notes

1. Spectatorship and Capture in King Kong

1. Jean-Luc Comolli and Jean Narboni.
2. See Claude Lévi-Strauss, "The Structural Study of Myth," in *Structural Anthropology* (New York: Anchor, 1967), pp. 202–228.
3. Brian Winston.
4. See Robin Wood, "An Introduction to the American Horror Film", from *The American Nightmare: Essays on the Horror Film* (Toronto: Festival of Festivals, 1979).
5. See, for instance, the argument of Calvin C. Hernton's *Sex and Racism in America* (New York: Grove Press, 1966) or Joel Kovel's *White Racism: A Psychohistory* (New York: Random House, 1971), or the chapter entitled "First Impressions: Initial English Confrontations with Africans," in Winthrop D. Jordan's *White over Black: American Attitudes Towards the Negro, 1550–1812* (New York: Norton, 1968).
6. Editors of *Cahiers du cinéma*, "John Ford's *Young Mr. Lincoln*," in *Movies and Methods*, Vol. 1, ed. Bill Nichols (Berkeley: University of California Press, 1976), p. 496.
7. See David MacDougall's article, "Beyond Observational Cinema," in *Principles of Visual Anthropology*, ed. Paul Hockings (The Hague: Mouton, 1975).
8. Orville Goldner and George E. Turner, *The Making of King Kong: The Story Behind a Film Classic* (New York: A.S. Barnes, 1975), p. 78.
9. Goldner and Turner, *The Making of King Kong*, p. 38.
10. Jordan, *White Over Black*, p. 491.
11. Goldner and Turner, *The Making of King Kong*, p. 68.
12. Robert Walker, "*King Kong* (1933)," *Cinema Texas: Program Notes*, vol. 7, no. 7 (September 12, 1974), p. 2.
13. Laura Mulvey, "Visual Pleasure and the Narrative Cinema," *Screen* 16, no. 3 (Autumn, 1975).
14. Daniel Dayan, "The Tutor-Code of Classical Cinema," in Nichols, *Movies and Methods*, Vol. 1, pp. 449–451.

151

15. Nick Browne, "The Spectator-in-the-Text: The Rhetoric of *Stage-coach*," *Film Quarterly* 34, no. 2 (Winter, 1975–1976).
16. Roland Barthes, *Mythologies*, trans. Annette Lavers (New York: Hill and Wang, 1972), pp. 151–152.
17. David MacDougall, "Prospects of the Ethnographic Film," *Film Quarterly*, vol. 23, no. 2 (Winter, 1969–1970).

6. Trimming Uncle Remus's Tales

1. Disney press release published on the reissue of *Song of the South*, November, 1986.
2. Leonard Maltin, *The Disney Films* (New York: Crown, 1973), p. 52.
3. Maltin, *Disney Films*, p. 78.
4. *Variety*, review of November 6, 1946; *New York Times*, review of December 8, 1946.
5. John Tumlin, "Introduction" to *Uncle Remus: Tales by Joel Chandler Harris* (Savannah: Beehive, 1974), p. xxiii, italics mine.
6. Joel Chandler Harris, "Introduction," *Uncle Remus: His Songs and His Sayings* (New York: D. Appleton, 1930), p. xvii.
7. See Nick Browne, "The Spectator-in-the-Text: The Rhetoric of *Stage-coach*," *Film Quarterly*, 34, no. 2, (Winter, 1975–76).
8. Maltin, *Disney Films*, p. 78; Disney press release.
9. Harris, *Uncle Remus*, p. 11.
10. Herman Hill, in the *Pittsburgh Courier*, quoted in Maltin, *Disney Films*, p. 78.
11. Robert Stam and Louise Spence, "Colonialism, Racism, and Representation: An Introduction," *Screen* 24, no. 2 (1983).
12. *New York Times*, December 14, 1946.

8. Playing the Changes

1. Amiri Baraka, *The Autobiography of Leroi Jones* (New York: Freundlich, 1984), p. 312. All subsequent references to this book in parentheses.

9. Images of Blacks in Black Independent Films

1. James Monaco, *How to Read a Film: The Art, Technology, Language, History, and Theory of Film and Media* (New York: Oxford University Press, 1981), p. 200.
2. Quoted in The Black Filmmaker Foundation, *Black Cinema* (New York: 1982), p. 39.
3. James R. Nesteby, *Black Images in American Films, 1896–1954: The Interplay Between Civil Rights and Film Culture* (New York: University

Press of America, 1982), p. 68, and passim, gives an exhaustive treatment of the entire early period of black filmmaking.

4. Thomas Cripps, *Black Film as Genre* (Bloomington: Indiana University Press, 1978), p. 69.

5. James Asendio, "History of Negro Motion Pictures," *International Photographer* (January 1940), p. 16.

Colin MacCabe is Professor of English at the University of Pittsburgh and Head of Research at the British Film Institute. Cornel West is Professor of Religion and Director of the Afro-American Studies Program at Princeton University.